The Ruth Experience

The Ruth Experience

UNCOVERING GOD'S PURPOSE FOR YOUR STORY

Kendra Roehl,
Kristin Demery
& Julie Fisk

Copyright

The Ruth Experience | Uncovering God's Purpose For Your Story

Copyright © 2015 Three Threads, LLC

Cover Design by DenaSwenson.com

Publishing and Design Services by MelindaMartin.me

Dedication

Thank you to our loving, long-suffering husbands who supported us on this wild writing adventure, to our parents for helping us become strong women like Ruth and Naomi, to the incredible women who agreed to share their stories with us in the hopes that it would change just one life, and to our Lord and Savior, Jesus Christ.

About the Authors

Julie Fisk was recently named a 2012 Minnesota Rising Star Attorney. A wife and mother of two, she serves as the children's ministry coordinator at her church, leads Bible studies and community groups, and speaks to women's groups.

Kendra Roehl received her bachelor's and master's degrees in social work and has worked for hospice programs, low-income housing, and the St. Cloud Veterans Affairs Medical Center. A mother of three, she currently stays at home, where she and her husband are foster and adoptive parents. Kendra has facilitated small groups on a variety of topics and co-led church groups. She co-directs community groups and is a member of the speaking team at her church.

Kristin Demery is a wife and mother of two with a background in journalism. Her news, business, and feature stories have been published in the *St. Cloud Times*, *ROI Business Magazine* and *USA Today*. Kristin has led Bible studies, co-led church groups, and managed a social network site for mothers. She is also working on her master's degree in English.

Contents

Introduction

The story of Ruth traces the journey of two very different, yet similar, women. Despite being from a different time and culture, Ruth and Naomi are not so different from you and me. In the story, we meet Naomi and Ruth shortly after each of them suffer devastating loss. In this book, we will walk alongside them as they cry out in anger at God, as they trust God despite their circumstances, and as they step forward in faith, relying on the promises of God. We will see how God answers their prayers and redeems their lives beyond their wildest dreams.

As we walk with Naomi and Ruth, we will explore how their journey parallels our own stories, despite the span of time and difference in cultures. We will challenge ourselves to examine our own lives as we hear stories of modern-day women who, through their faith in Christ, face and overcome infidelity, divorce, death, sacrifice, job loss, and infertility.

Just as Naomi and Ruth have a powerful story that transcends time and culture, we will explore how our own stories (including the good, the bad, and the ugly parts) have the power to transform the lives of women around us.

Finally, we offer practical ways to explore and share our own stories with the women around us in a way that is encouraging, uplifting, and that ultimately points other women to Christ's redeeming love.

Starting Over

But Naomi was firm: "Go back, my dear daughters. Why would you come with me? Do you suppose I still have sons in my womb who can become your future husbands? Go back, dear daughters—on your way, please! I'm too old to get a husband. Why, even if I said, 'There's still hope!' and this very night got a man and had sons, can you imagine being satisfied to wait until they were grown? Would you wait that long to get married again? No, dear daughters; this is a bitter pill for me to swallow—more bitter for me than for you. God has dealt me a hard blow."

—Ruth 1:11–13 (The Message)

The Death of a Dream

The story of Ruth and Naomi opens like so many stories in the Bible: someone is in the midst of a trial. In this case, Naomi has lost everything, including her husband, children, and all her earthly possessions. She is grieved, destitute, and embittered by her situation. And who could blame her? How many of us have stood in her shoes, with everything stripped away? Even more than the death of her family, Naomi's loss is the death of a dream. The dream of growing old with her husband, of watching her children have children of their own. For Naomi and for us, it is the dream of being surrounded by everything and everyone we value the most. So what does Naomi do? She decides to go back to what she knows, returning to the country of her youth.

It's interesting for us to imagine what may have gone through Naomi's mind as she and her two daughters-in-law left Moab and began to make their way back to Judea. Perhaps they wondered where they would stay, who would take them in, if they were even remembered by the people they used to know. Since widows in that era were often disregarded, ignored, or taken advantage of by others, her concerns must have been valid. With no father, husband, or brother to offer protection, Naomi and her daughters-in-law fit into one of the most vulnerable and disenfranchised groups of the day. In fact, throughout the Old Testament—in Malachi, Jeremiah, and Ezekiel, among others—God continually admonishes people to stop exploiting or taking advantage of the poor, widowed, and orphaned. In Psalm 68 (New Living Translation), he goes even further to call himself "father to the fatherless, defender of widows."

With each step pushing her further from the familiar and into the unknown, it seems likely that mixed with Naomi's uncertainty and fear were unfulfilled longings for her home in Moab, her life with her husband, and the joy of her children. In essence, a longing for things to have gone a different way. *Why couldn't he have lived? Why was his life not spared? Why did my sons have to die too?* Each step toward Bethlehem would have reminded Naomi of all that was gone, all that was lost. In her anger, she spoke, but not to God—not yet. Instead, she cried out to the two women with her, her daughters-in-law, "Go back! I have no hope of ever offering you any kind of security! Go back to your families, your gods, remarry. God has dealt me a hard blow." Truth be told, he had. And in the midst of her pain, it was difficult to understand why.

I (Julie) have always wanted a sister. My earliest memory is vivid: My mom and I were driving down a country road near our farm. I was three. As we crossed over a small bridge, my mom turned to me and told me excitedly that the new baby was going to be another brother. My little heart broke, and I burst into heart-wrenching sobs as only toddlers do. I wanted, more than anything, to have a sister.

In first grade, our teacher told us to imagine three things we would wish for and then asked us to draw our wishes on a piece of paper. I remember wiggling happily in my chair because I knew exactly what my wishes were: to be a princess, to live in a castle, and to have a sister. I excitedly pointed out that picture to my parents as it hung on the wall at open house and reminded them that I wanted a sister. Of all the art projects I did during my elementary-school years, that is the only one I remember.

I wanted a sister. I longed for a sister. I prayed for a sister. I didn't get a sister. I eventually realized I would never have a sister and set that dream aside. Long after childhood, I would still get an unexpected pang of longing when I saw two sisters share a knowing look or a laugh.

I met my "sisters" as an adult—although I didn't recognize them as such until years later. I have four of them. I met them in a Bible study. They have been in my life for nine years and have walked with me through great loss, greater joy, and everything in between. We pray for and with one another; we encourage and scold one another; and we tease, cheer, cry, laugh, and encourage one another through life. We've gone beyond the veneer of friendship into the realm of family. They are truly my sisters.

It was in a quiet moment of prayer that I realized my prayer for a sister had been answered. Reflecting on my desire to have a biological sister, my four dearest friends' faces came to mind along with several verses in Romans 8 defining Christians as being adopted into the family of God and made brothers and sisters in the body of Christ. Christians are repeatedly referred to as brothers and sisters throughout the New Testament. It was in that quiet moment that those verses came alive for me. I was gently reminded that God had already answered my deepest childhood longing to have a sister, above and beyond my wildest dreams, with four of the best adopted sisters in the body of Christ any woman has ever had. In that quiet moment of prayer I realized that my desire for a sister was answered long after my dream had died.

A Common Heartache

Naomi's story, though unique in its circumstances, is reflected in other stories throughout the Bible. From the depths of misery, Job's catastrophic loss of his family, livestock, home, and belongings culminated in a frank conversation with God. While scraping the open sores that afflict him with a broken piece of glass, Job reflected,

> *Why does God bother giving light to the miserable, why bother keeping bitter people alive, Those who want in the worst way to die, and can't, who can't imagine anything better than death, Who count the day of their death and burial the happiest day of their life? What's the point of life when it doesn't make sense, when God blocks all the roads to meaning? (Job 3:20–23 [MSG])*

Despite the thousands of years that separate their experiences from our own, many of us can relate to the feelings of loss, disappointment, and bitterness that both Naomi and Job expressed in the midst of difficulties. All it takes is a quick look around our world, our communities, and our own lives to know that life is not always fair, things don't always turn out the way we thought, and that most of us will at some point experience the death of a dream.

My husband and I (Kendra) have struggled for many years with infertility. While dating, we spoke often of our dream of having a large family. We knew from the start that we also planned to provide foster care, so when we did not get pregnant quickly, we decided to open our home to other children while also trying to have our own. That was several years ago, and in the meantime we have adopted one child through foster care, conceived and birthed one of our own, and are in the process of adopting a third child. It has been a trying process for us; we have had multiple doors close, including a miscarriage and failed adoption. And although there have been many blessings, I've also found myself crying out to the Lord, because just when I think our family is going to look one way, God shuts the door and moves us in another direction. It's been painful to give up the dream of what I envisioned for my family. But with all the heartache that has come, God has continued to prove his faithfulness through our ability to adopt children who originally came to us as foster children, through the surprise pregnancy of our son, and through the many children we have been blessed to parent as they transition back to their families through the foster care system. My husband and I now find ourselves with no expectations of what our family will look like in the future. We now completely trust that God will bring whatever children into our lives that he deems fit, at just the right time. Does this mean we'll never be heartbroken again? Absolutely not. It simply means we are learning, sometimes daily, to trust that God's plan for us and our family is better than anything we could have designed. When all is said and done, there's nowhere I'd rather be than pursuing God's plan for my family, rather than my own.

The point is not whether or not we will face tragedy and disappointment—Jesus said, "In this world, you will have trouble" for a reason—but rather, how you will react when it does. Like Naomi and Job, perhaps we should begin by simply allowing ourselves to be in an unknown place, not completely understanding what God has in store for us. Don't be afraid to ask yourself the questions that matter when you face the death of a dream: What do you do during this time of uncertainty? What or whom do you believe? And where do you turn for comfort?

Linda's Story

It was at her daughter's wedding that life as Linda knew it fell apart.

It wasn't the first time. She and her husband, Russ, met while working at a restaurant as teenagers, and over the years the wife and mother of two had already faced her share of challenges.

First, their house burned down.

"That was very devastating because we were very young," she said, recalling how she grabbed her baby and raced outside. She remembers watching her home explode and thinking there would never be anything worse than that experience.

"And then there was," she said, "only one year later, the cancer came on. That was devastating, and you think, 'Nothing else can beat that.'"

But her greatest challenge began at her youngest daughter's wedding, during what was supposed to be a happy occasion, when a man walked over to her eldest daughter and asked if she knew that her father—Linda's husband—was having an affair with his wife. Worse, the woman was Linda's best friend.

Reeling, they quickly defused the situation, but Linda's outward composure proved to be the calm before the storm. As they left the wedding, the emotions she had suppressed came boiling to the surface. Overcome with anger, she threw a hot cup of coffee in Russ's face.

But once they arrived home, they played the role of a happily married couple for the out-of-town guests staying in their home for the next two days. On the third day, they sat down for a long discussion where she demanded the unvarnished truth. Despite having had suspicions about his behavior, she was blindsided by the news that the affair had lasted two and a half years.

"Things happen and you backtrack and think, 'Why was I so blind? Why was I so naïve? And why didn't I listen to my gut feeling?'" she said.

In the year leading up to the confrontation at the wedding, she had begun to wonder about the nights he would stay up late and be on the phone in their office, but he would always brush off her concerns. And between their busy schedule and her exhaustion from being a daycare provider, she didn't have the energy or inclination to pursue it further. Though she instinctively knew something was wrong, an affair wasn't something she had even considered.

For Linda, starting over in her marriage meant reorganizing their priorities as a couple. Instead of focusing solely on their children and grandchildren, they began to make more time for each other.

"Russ and I needed something in our marriage to wake us up and to show us how important we are to each other—not the kids, not your job, not the church—and I could never get Russ there, but God had a plan," she said.

She also trusted and claimed the words to Jeremiah 29:11 (New International Version): "'For I know the plans I have for you,' declares the Lord, 'plans to prosper you and not to harm you, plans to give you hope and a future.'"

"I stood on that verse. He knew it was going to happen, he was going to make me strong and now I see all the ways he was preparing me," she said. "It has drawn our marriage very close. I don't know what else would have done that."

Starting over also meant putting God first, giving her a deeper, richer walk with Christ.

"For so long, I felt like I had God, but I always relied on Russ and my kids for my happiness," she said. "I always relied on Russ for everything, and it was like God was saying, 'No, you need to rely on me. I am your comforter, your friend—your best friend. I am here for you.'"

"It changed me a lot. There's no one like my God. There's nobody, there's nothing I want more than him," she said and paused. "I love my daughters; I love my grandkids. But my children sometimes disappoint me, my husband sometimes disappoints me, my extended family sometimes disappoints me, I disappoint me—but God never does, and he never closes the door on me. I can't imagine my life without him."

Conclusion

The true test for both Linda and Naomi was not what happened to them when the things they held dear were stripped away, but how they were transformed through their loss. It's through challenges, hardships, and difficulties that we decide what we will cling to and what we will let go. The story of Naomi opens with a woman being pressed, presumably beyond what she can bear, in order to show us what God can do in the life of someone who chooses to follow him when the road home is challenging. Only where there has been great loss can God show us his great gain. And so our story opens with Naomi making a choice to journey to the life and the home she knows, to return to the God of her youth. Through this, God reveals to her and to us what he is able to do through those who are battered, even embittered, by life.

Job, like Linda, found that although he experienced great loss, he experienced even greater restoration. God didn't just return his family and fortune, but instead gave him twice as much as before! It wasn't just his resources that God restored, but his family. The Bible describes how Job "lived to see four generations of his children and grandchildren. Then he died, an old man who had lived a long, full life." (Job 42:16-17 [NLT])

Although we may not always understand *why* things happen to us, we can rest assured that God *will* use all things for our benefit and his glory. We know this because there is nothing that indicates Naomi, Job, or even Linda were anything more than "common" people of their day. Matthew 10:29–31 (NLT) tells us, "What is the price of two sparrows—one copper coin? But not a single sparrow can fall to the ground without your Father knowing it. And the very hairs on your head are all numbered. So don't be afraid; you are more valuable to God than a whole flock of sparrows." The promise we can glean from Job's story and Linda's testimony is that God cares about our circumstances no matter who we are. He is willing to be with us and walk with us when we are facing the death of a dream. He may not move us out of the unknown as quickly as we'd like, but we can rest assured that he has a plan and is capable to move us to a new place, a *restored* place, in his timing.

Prayer

Lord, you know intimately the disappointments, the broken dreams, and the tragedies we've walked through in our lives. As we take this moment to hand them over to you, one by one, meet us in that place of surrender in the midst of uncertainty. May your quiet peace gently surround and settle over us as we wait. Bring to our minds scripture on which we can firmly stand as we walk daily in the assurance that you are beside us, you know what lies ahead, and you will be our unfailing rock, even when our children, spouses, families, friends, coworkers, and humankind fail us. May you wipe away our tears from unfulfilled childhood longings, the heartbreak of infertility, the fear of cancer, the devastation of betrayed relationships, and all of the unspoken pain we've experienced. Help us run to you in the midst of our pain and our tears and wait quietly in your presence while you restore what has been lost. Amen.

Your Turn

Read Ruth 1:1–13. At the close of each chapter, you will find a portion of the book of Ruth to read on your own and questions to further your understanding. The questions can be done individually or in a group setting. Each question is meant to help you begin to recognize your own story and the ways that God has been present in your life and circumstances. By the end of the book, you will also have read the entire book of Ruth.

1. *Have you ever found yourself in a place where you asked God why a circumstance or difficulty was happening in your life? Explain.*

_____

_____

_____

2. *How have you experienced the death of a dream in your own life?*

_____

_____

_____

3. In the chapter, we discussed the idea that through trials we find out what we are willing to hang on to and what we will let go. What have you found that was helpful for you to cling to during difficult times? What did you choose to let go of?

_____

_____

_____

4. "Only where there has been great loss can God show us his great gain." Do you agree with this statement? What examples do you have from your own life that illustrate this point?

_____

_____

_____

5. *Psalm 73:25–26 [NLT] says, "Whom have I in heaven but you? I desire you more than anything on earth. My health may fail, and my spirit may grow weak, but God remains the strength of my heart; he is mine forever." God wants nothing more than for our desires to line up with his, our heart to beat in tune to his heart. Sometimes he reveals his truth to us and we change or let go of certain things, and sometimes he allows circumstances to change that force us to let go. Have you seen times in your life where your desires didn't line up with God's desires for you? How did they change? Were you able to say, as David did, "I desire you more than anything on earth"?*

_____

_____

_____

2

Getting Honest with God

But she said, "Don't call me Naomi; call me Bitter. The Strong One has dealt me a bitter blow. I left here full of life, and God has brought me back with nothing but the clothes on my back. Why would you call me Naomi? God certainly doesn't. The Strong One ruined me."

—*Ruth 1:20–21 (MSG)*

Honesty with God sounds like such a simple thing. He knows everything anyway, so why not tell him, right? Yet sometimes it can seem so difficult. I (Julie) was twenty-seven years old when my dear friend Kate died. She was twenty-eight, had two young children, and was a beautiful woman with more grace, poise, maturity, and faith in God than anyone I have ever met. Kate fought and repeatedly overcame cancer in a variety of amazing and inexplicable ways. I was absolutely convinced that Kate was going to beat cancer, live to an old age, and share her amazing testimony with thousands of other people. I knew God was using her, and I knew he was going to heal her. I had no doubt as to how the story was going to end.

And then she died. I was angry, sad, and shaken in my faith. After two months of faking it through church, I confronted God one afternoon. I was honest about my anger and great sadness at losing someone I loved, someone I thought God should have healed. And after my one-sided, out-loud conversation with God, I realized I had to choose to either trust God to have a bigger plan despite her death or stop trusting him and walk away. Choosing to trust and believe God's promises, I clung to Romans 8:28 (NLT)—"And we know that God causes everything to work together for the good of those who love God and are called according to his purpose"—and prayed that I might see him use Kate's life and death in a way that changed lives.

In the days that followed, I woke every morning choosing to trust God and reminding him of my prayer. Do you know that I have had the privilege of sharing Kate's story with people who never met her starting that same week and continuing countless times over the years since her death? The opportunities arose in the strangest ways, and I never missed a chance to tell someone about Jesus through Kate's story because I knew that opportunity was the answer to my Romans 8:28 prayer! Less than a month ago, more than eight years after her death, I shared Kate's story with a woman over a cup of coffee at Perkins.

God has allowed me glimpses of Kate's great legacy, even as it continues today—through a nonprofit foundation, her siblings, her parents, her children, her husband, the Bible study she started, and even through people she never actually met. God has used her legacy in ways that leave me shaking my head in wonderment! I still wish God had answered my prayer to heal Kate differently; however, I will also tell you that God can handle our anger when we hand it to him while trusting him and, sometimes, he blesses us with a glimpse of his greater plan as a way to ease our pain.

Like Julie's anger and disappointment over Kate's death, Naomi also struggled with her emotions and her ability to trust in God despite her circumstances. Her husband was dead. Her two sons were dead. In a culture in which women typically must rely upon men to survive, Naomi not only mourned the loss of her family, she mourned the loss of her once-secure future, now stripped away. Naomi returned to her homeland in a desperate situation, and it showed.

In fact, Naomi's personality was so markedly different that when she returned to her hometown of Bethlehem, people asked in astonishment, "Is this Naomi?" Her public outcry over what she perceived as God's mistreatment—"Don't call me Naomi! Call me Bitter…the Strong One has ruined me"—would have been as shocking as someone today standing up in the middle of a church sermon, angrily laying out how God has wronged them, and then storming out of the service. To others, she seemed like a different person, an idea she echoes in her self-loathing wish to change her name from Naomi, which means "pleasant" or "beautiful," to "Bitter." When God changes names in the Bible, he does it to establish someone's growth or to show favor. As humans, we go the opposite way, distorting something of beauty (ourselves!) in reaction to our circumstances. Naomi's renaming reflects the ugliness of her feelings.

It might be easy at this point in the story to become critical of Naomi and her apparent disrespect for God, but instead of fulfilling our expectations, God doesn't reprimand Naomi. Instead, God honors her willingness to be honest with him by giving her the space she needs.

Three Reasons Why Honesty with God Matters

1. It Reveals the Familiar Nature of Our Relationship

Doesn't it seem like we become most angry those we are closest to? We have no problem telling our husband we are upset when he shows up late for supper—again—or forgets to take out the garbage. Instead, it's usually when interacting with acquaintances like our neighbors, the woman in the checkout line at the grocery store, or our child's teacher that we feel the need to pretend everything is perfect. When asked how we're doing, we quickly smile and say we're fine, regardless of how we truly feel. It reminds me of how my mom used to answer the phone with a sweet "hello" while shooting my sisters and me a scathing look of death for being too noisy.

It is no different with God. Honesty with God is a measure of our familiarity with him. It shows that we have a relationship with him, and that even in the midst of a struggle, we are willing to risk being honest because we know that he can be trusted. In return, God is not put off by our honesty. He is not vulnerable to our criticism, and he can handle our concerns. It is much like our relationship with our spouse—if we never told them what we were thinking or feeling, what sort of relationship would we have? Sure, everything on the surface would look good, but there would be no real intimacy, no connection, no substance. Only with honesty do we allow vulnerability, and that is where Naomi finds herself—speaking from a place of pain, lashing out from her grief, being vulnerable before God. It is as though she's saying "You've hurt me!" and is waiting for his reply.

2. It Shows God's Willingness to Honor and Listen to Our True Feelings

Despite her angry words, God did not reprimand Naomi for her honesty. Instead, Naomi and others like her throughout the Bible are honored for their sincerity. King David, for instance, was known for his intimacy with God, yet in Psalm 55:4–5 (NLT) he is starkly honest: "My heart pounds in my chest. The terror of death assaults me. Fear and trembling overwhelm me, and I can't stop shaking...But I will call on God, and the Lord will rescue me."

God loves us enough to honor the sincerity of our hearts and the emotions we're willing to reveal to him through our honesty. It is only when we are dishonest with ourselves and God as a result of pride or arrogance that God chooses to chastise us for our behavior. Despite Jesus's penchant for mingling with sinners, it was only the Pharisees—the so-called righteous, religious leaders of the day—who were criticized for their lies and deceit. In the Bible, Jesus speaks harshly of their dishonesty:

> You're hopeless, you religion scholars and Pharisees! Frauds! You burnish the surface of your cups and bowls so they sparkle in the sun, while the insides are maggoty with your greed and gluttony. Stupid Pharisee! Scour the insides, and then the gleaming surface will mean something. (Matt. 23:25–26 [MSG])

Jesus goes so far as to call these self-righteous men "frauds"— not because of their position, but because of their inability to be honest with God and others. It's a warning for us as well, a caution that dishonesty with God and those around us can lead to pride in ourselves or in our own abilities. It creates distance between us and others, and just as importantly, it creates distance between us and God. It removes our ability to be vulnerable with others. It says, "I don't need to tell you what I'm really feeling, that I'm really hurt." Instead of being honest, we throw up defenses, we give someone the silent treatment, or we say we are fine when we're really not. And, in turn, we act as frauds.

The dictionary defines *pride* as "a high or inordinate opinion of one's own dignity, importance, merit, or superiority, whether as cherished in the mind or as displayed in bearing, conduct, etc." We hold tightly to our pride rather than admitting our true feelings, fearing that our openness will result in the loss of our dignity. Many years ago, I (Kendra) attended a women's conference with some of the women from my church. There was a woman in our group who was new to Christianity who shared very openly—perhaps too openly, I thought disparagingly—about her past life experiences and relationships with men. I thought to myself, "I don't share like that. It must be because I'm a more mature Christian." Immediately, I heard God's voice whisper to me, "No, you're just proud." I was taken aback but felt immediately convicted. In the years since, I have realized that my inability to open up to others was not a measure of the maturity of my faith but rather a desire to cover up my own flaws and imperfections. It takes courage to be the kind of person who is willing to share with others, to be vulnerable and admit to weaknesses. It is worth remembering that the antonym to *pride* is *humility*. When we come in humility, honestly laying out our complaints, our hurts, and our anger before the Lord, he honors us.

3. God Hears, and Is Moved by It

There are many examples in scripture of God attending to the cry of people. Hannah cried out to the Lord because of her barrenness, and in Exodus, the Israelites "groaned in their slavery" while held captive In Egypt. Hagar, alone and pregnant in the wilderness, cried out and was answered by the angel of the Lord. In each case, God heard and responded to his people. Even today, he listens for honesty in people, their lives and situations, and he is moved by their pain. In Psalm 34:18 (NLT), it says, "The Lord is close to the brokenhearted; he rescues those whose spirits are crushed." As we cry out to him, he hears. It's not just those we recognize as having a voice in the world—the politicians, the leaders, the wealthy—who are heard by God. He hears the cry of all. In Naomi's case, he heard a lowly widow, returning home with nothing but the clothes on her back and her daughter-in-law in tow and was moved to her rescue.

Despite the time and distance between us and Naomi, her story is not so unlike our own. It's as if God is whispering to us in the midst of our pain: "I am near, your life matters, and I can rescue you." The question we must answer is, will our honesty turn to vulnerability, which in turn becomes trust and faith? It was a choice Naomi faced, and it is the same choice we must face as well.

Kristin's Story

Kristin's oldest sister Katrina was diagnosed with breast cancer at age twenty-three and, for the next five years, had an off-and-on battle with the disease.

"I loved her innate sense of beauty and grace," Kristin said. "Despite the fact that I was probably an annoying baby sister, she never made me feel overlooked or unwanted."

By the time Kristin was in college, Katrina was still fighting the disease, her hospital stays becoming more frequent and for longer periods of time.

One day, Kristin got a phone call at work: Katrina was at a store a few doors down and had collapsed in the dressing room. Kristin raced to see her, oblivious to the cool day and the wind whipping around her, concentrating instead on not tripping in her high heels and keeping her wayward skirt from flying into her face. When she got to the store, Katrina was lying on the floor in the dressing room, her head cradled in a stranger's lap. The stranger glanced up at Kristin even as she continued to croon softly to Katrina, who was still suffering the aftershocks of losing consciousness in a strange place.

Kristin asked the store employees to call the ambulance, then knelt down and gripped Katrina's hand as they waited for help to arrive.

"Everyone else in the family—our parents, my brother-in-law Jim, and our sister Kendra—was out of town," Kristin said. "As I held her hand and waited for the ambulance, I had never felt so alone or so scared."

Trying to stay calm, she began to simply talk to fill the space. She watched Katrina rally enough to laugh at her inane jokes and her impression of how she resembled a penguin in her race to get to the store, running with her hands at her sides to hold her skirt in place while her heels flopped on the sidewalk.

Her heart broke, she said, when she found out that when Katrina passed out on the floor, other people stepped over her in their haste to get in and out of the dressing room, rather than stopping to help.

"Finding out that Katrina had fallen and not gotten help right away, I was so enraged," Kristin said. "I felt like screaming. I felt like throwing up. I felt like hitting something, or lashing out in a way that would hurt someone the way I was hurting."

She did none of those things. Instead, Kristin started to get angry to God. To see her sister reduced by cancer—suffering the indignity of being ignored and overlooked in her pain—she felt it keenly, and it burned.

But in front of others, she pretended to be fine. God knew she was angry, but no one else did.

"I've been a Christian nearly my whole life, so I'm used to hearing all of the clichés we say when problems come up in our lives," she said. "God has a plan. God has a purpose. God's ways are not our ways. God loves us. Logically, I knew that it was true, but in my heart I felt differently. If God cared, why was Katrina sick?"

That fall, it came to a head. At a Christian college retreat, she and her friends sat in the audience and listened to a speaker talk about confessing sins to each other and to God. They were then challenged to do so—in front of everyone.

"Immediately, my heart started pounding, and I felt sick to my stomach," Kristin said. "I have an extreme fear of public speaking that I've struggled with for years. I thought, 'Surely God wouldn't ask me to get up in front of a room full of people and confess something, would he?'"

It was then that she felt a voice—the Holy Spirit—whisper quietly, "You need to confess your anger over Katrina's cancer."

"I thought, 'What? What anger?' Surely God didn't mean for me to lay down my pride, face the risk of exposure to all these people for something I wasn't even willing admit to myself," Kristin said. "In that moment, I felt myself on the edge of a precipice. I could continue to deny my anger, lie to myself, God, and everyone else—sitting self-righteously in my chair and pretending everything was fine—or I could admit the anger and move on."

Trembling, she began to walk up the aisle, stepping on to the stage and waiting for a turn at the microphone. Tears streaming down her face, she finally admitted her anger to others.

"As the words tumbled out of my mouth, I felt lighter and lighter," she said. "Finally, I could be honest. God knew I was angry and bitter, but my honesty with him and with others was the tipping point. God could handle my anger, and he loved me anyway."

And the embarrassment she thought she might experience after her revelation to a room full of people? When she walked off the stage, instead of the rejection she expected, Kristin found herself enveloped in warmth and love as friends and strangers alike held her close, prayed for her, and cried with her. God honored her honesty, and though Kristin says she still struggled with anger after that day, she believed God would hold her when she raged and be there afterward to love her, just as her friends had done.

It was during that experience that Isaiah 43:1–4 (MSG) became an essential promise:

> *But now, God's Message, the God who made you in the first place, Jacob, the One who got you started, Israel: "Don't be afraid, I've redeemed you. I've called your name. You're mine. When you're in over your head, I'll be there with you. When you're in rough waters, you will not go down. When you're between a rock and a hard place, it won't be a dead end—Because I am God, your personal God, The Holy of Israel, your Savior. I paid a huge price for you: all of Egypt, with rich Cush and Seba thrown in! That's how much you mean to me! That's how much I love you! I'd sell off the whole world to get you back, trade the creation just for you."*

When Katrina died a few years later, Kristin said the words from Isaiah became even more important.

"One of the analogies people mention when they talk about grief is how it is like a wave, crashing over you," Kristin said. "You think you're fine and then, whoosh, it crashes over you when you least expect it. This passage helped—knowing that even though I felt like I was drowning in those waves of grief, God wouldn't let me go down."

Conclusion

Although we don't know the exact conversation that happened between Naomi and God after her tirade in the town square, it seems probable that just as in Kristin's testimony, her willingness to publicly proclaim her true feelings aloud was the start of her healing process. Though the way she expressed herself may not be the same way that you or I would choose to, the point is that she did it. She revealed her pain to God, and it is from that point on that she was able to move to a place of greater faith and, ultimately, trust in God's ways and his plans for her life.

Prayer

Lord, draw near to us as we bring you our anger, hurt, and sorrow over our past, our present circumstances, and our loved ones. Thank you that you are a safe place to express our deepest regrets, our biggest fears, and our greatest losses. Surround us with your presence as we pour out our hearts about cancer, illness, financial ruin, abuse, and those hurts that we have buried so deeply within our souls that, until this moment, we dared not speak them aloud. Lord, be with us as we weep over childhoods lost, precious friends and family who have died, and circumstances that seem overwhelmingly against us. As we cry out, pull us close. Remind us that you are big enough to hear our hearts' cries without flinching, you are merciful to wrap us in your arms while we weep in anguish, and that you will not forsake us or leave us in our times of greatest need. Help us to bring our secret torments to you and leave them with you. Heal the deep wounds of our hearts with your great love. You, Lord, respond to the downtrodden, the brokenhearted, and the destitute. Continue to reveal yourself to us so that we would know you intimately, that our relationship with you would grow deeper, and that our trust in you would be complete, no matter the storm that rages around us. Amen.

Your Turn

Read Ruth 1:14–22.

1. *Do you find it easy or difficult to be honest with others? Are you willing to be honest in all of your interactions, or is your honesty reserved only for those closest to you?*

_____

_____

_____

2. *Do you find it easy or difficult to be honest with God? Is there anything holding you back from surrendering your true thoughts and feelings to him?*

_____

_____

_____

3. Proverbs 14:2 [MSG] says that "*an honest life shows respect for God; a degenerate life is a slap in his face.*" The dictionary defines degenerate as someone or something that "*falls below a normal or desirable level in physical, mental, or moral qualities; deteriorate: or to diminish in quality, especially from a former state of coherence, balance, integrity.*" This verse seems to imply that an honest life is an active life, not one that is stagnant or degenerates by moving backward. How have you seen honesty move you forward in your relationship with God and in life? Are there areas where you have become stagnant that you need to address?

_____

_____

_____

3

Trust in the Midst of Trial

Naomi said to her daughter-in-law, "Why, God bless that man! God hasn't quite walked out on us after all! He still loves us, in bad times as well as good!" Naomi went on, "That man, Ruth, is one of our circle of covenant redeemers, a close relative of ours!"

—Ruth 2:20 (MSG)

What happens when life makes a wrong turn or circumstances look impossible? Do we take matters into our own hands and attempt to "fix" the problem, or do we bring it to God? Oftentimes, how we react in these situations reveals how much we trust God. It's easy to trust God when everything is sunshine and lollipops. When life gets difficult, we pull the situation into our own hands, worry, obsess, and run in circles in a vain attempt to solve the problem by ourselves. That is not what God asks us to do. God asks us to trust him, even with the hard stuff.

Trusting in God's Promises

Although Naomi did not have the benefit of New Testament accounts of Jesus to rely upon when trusting God, Naomi knew

God through Old Testament scripture, the laws and codes set out by Moses and the leaders of the Israelites, and through sacrifice, prayer, and worship. She was raised in a culture whose belief in and worship of God was central to their very identity and was what set them apart from other cultures. Naomi would have known and worshiped God from her earliest memories.

Yet if Naomi had let her circumstances dictate her trust in God, her story would have ended differently. On the surface, Ruth and Naomi's return from Moab to Naomi's hometown appears grim: they are destitute, with no steady source of income, food, or resources. One of the few social welfare programs available was the opportunity to walk the barley and wheat fields behind the harvesters and pick up the few stray stalks of grain that fell to the ground or were missed in the harvest. It was hot, dirty work and women risked being raped.

It was in this environment that Ruth set out to glean in the fields in the second chapter of Ruth. She unknowingly began to gather barley in the fields of a man named Boaz. Boaz is identified as a godly man who immediately notices Ruth. Despite knowing that she is a low-status Moabitess (and therefore not one of God's chosen people) and a widow, he shows her mercy. He invites her to eat lunch with him and his servants. He instructs his servants to leave extra grain for her to gather. He sends her home with an extra portion of grain. And he instructs her to glean only in his fields so that she would be protected from harm. He goes above and beyond any general duty to a widow gleaning in his field. Ruth rushes home to tell Naomi of their good fortune in meeting Boaz. Naomi, despite her anger and disappointment in their circumstances, recognizes that something the world would consider a coincidence is actually God's hand at work. In other words, she trusts God. It is Naomi's reaction to Ruth's story that forever alters the lives of these two women and, ultimately, history. In the second chapter of Ruth, verse 20 (MSG), Naomi says, "Why, God bless that man! God hasn't quite walked out on us after all! He still loves us, in bad times as well as good." Without Naomi's knowledge of God's promises and her trust in him, this story would just be another story of two widows struggling to survive. Yet it is because of Naomi's trust and Ruth's faithfulness to step out before seeing the end result that we recognize them not only as women portrayed in the Bible, but as women who are in the very lineage of Jesus Christ.

Several years ago, my husband and I (Kendra) faced a devastating job loss. Although I enjoyed my job as a full-time social worker, my desire was to stay home with my children. In fact, my husband and I spent the first several months of my pregnancy planning for me to quit my job when the baby, our second child, arrived. One day when I was about six months pregnant with our son, my husband came home early from work. I immediately felt that something was wrong. He asked if we could speak privately in our bedroom, away from the kids, where he then told me that he had been let go that day. Feeling panicked, I immediately began searching for job opportunities for my husband. Over the next few weeks, I repeatedly gave the situation over to the Lord in prayer, only to take it back. Because of my inability to trust God, I would vacillate from having peace about the situation and being kind to my husband to feeling panicked and lashing out at him. Finally, he calmly told me, "Kendra, be mad at me or not, either way is fine, but please stop going back and forth. I don't know what to expect from you." In that moment, I knew I wasn't being fair to him. I finally had to decide to truly surrender my will to God and allow him to be in control—which, for me, meant no more job-searching for my husband. Instead, each morning, I prayed a blessing over my husband and that God would change my heart toward him. Eventually God did, and my husband had the confidence to go out and find a new way to provide for our family.

The Bible is filled with stories of people who trusted God during the hardest, scariest, most difficult times of their lives. It's easy to gloss over these stories and dismiss them as not applicable to our lives or our circumstances because they occurred so long ago. But the story of Jarius illustrates how little life has changed in the last two thousand years.

Unequivocal Trust

Jarius is introduced after the disciples have been following Jesus for almost a year. As the lay leader of a synagogue, he would have been in charge of the building and administrative tasks. Jarius was probably a well-known man in his community and likely held a privileged position. Although the story of Jarius appears in the biblical accounts of Matthew, Mark, and Luke, our focus is on the fifth chapter of Mark.

The story opens as Jesus steps off a boat and is immediately surrounded by a large crowd of people. Jarius pushes his way through the crowd as he tries to get to Jesus. He believes Jesus has power to heal people, and he is desperate to reach him. I can imagine him: Out of breath, panicking, knowing there is not much time as he throws himself at the feet of Jesus and begs, "My dear daughter is at death's door. Come and lay hands on her so she will get well and live" (Mark 5: 22 [MSG]). At the worst moment of this man's life, Jesus literally shows up. Great, right? As readers, we think Jesus is going to run to Jarius's house and heal his daughter. She'll be just fine. Isn't that what we expect of God when things get hard? Sometimes Jesus does do that—he immediately intervenes. But how do we react when Jesus doesn't immediately rush to our aid? Do we trust him, or do we try to do it on our own?

In Jarius's case, Jesus agrees to see his daughter, but as the story unfolds, we notice that Jesus does not rush and, in fact, gets distracted. As Jesus walks toward Jarius's house, the crowd continues to surge around him, bumping and jostling him. What must Jarius have thought as he watched Jesus slowly making his way through a crowd that wouldn't clear the way for an emergency? I know what I would do: Grab Jesus by the hand and pull him as fast as I could to the bedside of my child. I would elbow my way through that crowd. There would be no stopping, no consideration for anyone else. I would not be a nice woman; I would be a mom desperate to save my child and good luck to anyone who gets in my way. Jesus, however, did not react in a way we might expect. He didn't yell at the crowd to clear a path, elbow anyone to get through, or run. Jesus was not in a hurry.

For Jarius, the story gets worse: A woman with a chronic illness manages to touch a corner of Jesus's garment, hoping that simply touching his clothes will heal her disease. Jesus immediately stops, realizing someone has touched him. He begins searching, calling out, demanding to know who touched him. The woman eventually gathers the courage to step forward only to collapse at the feet of Jesus, spilling out the story of her life and confessing her illness that, in her culture, made her unclean and forbade her from touching anyone. She broke the law by daring to touch Jesus. Jesus, in the midst of the crowd, in the middle of an emergency, gazes into this woman's soul and changes her life by telling her that she has been healed by her faith. Her life, lived on society's fringes for years, has been redeemed and made whole.

Many of us are familiar with the story of the unclean woman's healing, but I wonder if we have ever stopped to think of Jarius as he witnessed that moment. What did the father of a beloved, dying child think as Jesus conversed with a person considered unclean, a societal outcast, someone considered to be a waste of a life? Was Jarius angry, impatient, or frustrated? And then it comes, the news that forever breaks the heart of a parent: As Jesus is still talking to the woman, messengers from Jarius's house approach to say, "Your daughter is dead. Why bother the Teacher anymore?" We are not told how Jarius responded, if he was overcome by shock or angered by the delays that left his child dead. How frustrating it must have been for Jarius, as it is for us today, when we try to fix an impossible situation ourselves only to fall short.

Jesus, overhearing the news, tells Jarius, "Don't listen to them, just trust me." Jarius was at a crossroads. Although we, two thousand years later, know Jesus had the power to raise people from the dead, Jarius did not have that advantage. Jesus didn't raise Lazarus from the dead until later in his ministry. Jesus asked Jarius to trust him despite the fact that everything he knew—all earthly experiences, medical knowledge, and scientific evidence—said it was too late, his daughter was dead. Jarius had a choice to say a public "yes" to Jesus and continue toward his house or decline and walk away. In that moment, Jarius chose to trust.

Ultimately, his trust was well-placed. Jesus raised his daughter from the dead.

Trust Despite Our Circumstances

Although we can appreciate it, the happy ending isn't the point. The point is that Jarius, in the midst of crisis, trusted Jesus with the life of his beloved daughter. How do we translate this into our own lives? At what point do we let go of a situation and trust God, even when we know that God might stroll along, stop to help someone else, or answer our prayer in a way that maybe we didn't expect? I (Julie) am the intensely independent oldest of three siblings. Growing up, I was the self-appointed protector of my two younger brothers. I challenged the school bus bullies in elementary school, acted as a mother hen to my brothers whether they liked it or not, and the original reason I became a lawyer was because I wanted to make sure I could always protect my family and the people I loved. You recognize the problem with this, right? I mistakenly thought that "I" could protect my family. If only "I" was smart enough, if "I" knew the legal system enough, if "I" was powerful enough, then "I" could keep other people from hurting those I loved. Although I loved Jesus as a child, it was as a young adult that I developed a relationship with him. It was then that I began realizing "I" was not the answer to protecting those I loved. I needed to entrust those I loved to Jesus. And I did that, kind of. You see, I continued to reserve a secret spot in my heart in which I believed that "I" could protect my family. I didn't realize at the time that I was holding back from fully trusting Jesus. I didn't recognize it, but Jesus did.

I continued to "mostly" trust God until my brother, Jake, informed me that he was going to spend a year in a third-world country as a missionary engineering a water project. I was okay with that, until he and his wife got there and realized the situation was far more dangerous than they had anticipated. Marauding bandits were breaking into homes within the missionary compound every night without fear because there was no police force to stop them. On top of the general violence of the region, Jake's work on the water project angered a neighboring village to the point that they threatened to attack the missionary compound, and made personal threats to Jake and his wife. We communicated through Skype, and although I loved our visits, it was difficult to turn off that computer screen knowing I was leaving loved ones in a scary situation halfway across the world. As the situation deteriorated, I distinctly remember one late night in which I tried desperately to think of a way to help my brother through my own resources. Could I contact the embassy? Hire armed men to fight back? Go and take on the bad guys myself? As my ideas for rescue grew outlandish, I finally realized there was absolutely nothing I could do to help him. My law degree was worthless in that country; I was powerless to do anything. It was in that moment, as I sobbed facedown into the carpet, that I was gently reminded that my only option was to trust Jesus and to pray. And so I did. That night, I handed two people I love dearly to Jesus, without holding on to the secret idea of rescuing them myself. Finally letting go of that secret hope was painful but necessary if I was going to grow in my relationship with Jesus. Despite the uncertainty of the situation, my family and I spent weeks trusting Jesus and praying for his intervention. The day my brother and sister-in-law were safely delivered out of that situation, I wept. In fact, I had to close my office door at work for most of the day because I could not stop weeping unexpectedly. The day they arrived on my doorstep, I wept again. Having the opportunity to hug my brother again was an answer to a prayer that I had completely and unequivocally surrendered to Jesus.

How is it that Jarius was able to trust Jesus when he said to ignore what others were telling him? It is simple. Jarius knew Jesus enough to know that he had the ability to heal people. After all, he had just witnessed Jesus heal a woman from a chronic illness. Webster's dictionary defines the word *trust* as "assured reliance on the character, ability, strength, or truth of someone or something." As women, we build trust with one another through relationship. We do not immediately trust someone we have just met. We build trust as we spend time, energy, and experiences together. We test our new friend in small ways to see if she follows through on her promises, holds our small secrets in confidence, and is a safe person in which to share our deep hurts, dreams, and prayers. It is only after we have developed relationship that we trust.

It is the same with Jesus. We have to have a relationship before we can fully trust him. We have to see his personality as it is revealed through scripture before we will let him heal our hurts, hold our loved ones, and let him into our hearts without condition, without reservation. Only then will we be able to give up our secret plans to step in if he does not.

Jenny's Story

The proverbial bomb dropped on a Monday. Jenny and her youth pastor husband, Carl, had just returned from a weekend leadership conference where they felt refreshed, reaffirmed in their ministry, and excited about the future.

Imagine their surprise when Carl met the senior pastor at a local coffee shop Monday morning only to find out that, suddenly and inexplicably, he was being let go. More than that, the church wanted him to tell others he was leaving voluntarily.

"We couldn't tell anyone that we were fired, we had to say we resigned," Jenny later recalled. "We couldn't even tell our friends the real reason that we were leaving."

Stunned, Carl and Jenny were unsure what to do next. With a mortgage and two young sons, they felt overwhelmed: Should Carl find a new job in the ministry or leave it entirely? Should he go back to school? Should they stay in the area or move away?

Almost overnight, they decided to move to Minnesota and live with Jenny's family while they sorted things out. Within the space of a week, Jenny went from a comfortable existence to living in her parents' basement and sleeping on a blow-up mattress.

As they got in the moving truck, Jenny felt like Lot's wife, struggling not to look back on what they were leaving behind.

"I remember feeling sick to my stomach driving away," she said. "We had to move, our house wasn't sold, we had to leave all our stuff in our house that we had only been in for a couple of years. I had to leave it all."

During the long hours spent in the moving van, Jenny focused on trusting God despite their circumstances, recalling the words to Proverbs 3:5-6 (NIV 1984): "Trust in the Lord with all your heart and lean not on your own understanding; in all your ways acknowledge him and he will make your paths straight."

"Trusting God is not always easy, and often it's something you have to pray and seek God to help you with it daily and sometimes hourly," she said. "He had to tell me that looking back on everything I thought I was losing wasn't putting my full trust in God that he would take care of us."

Within a couple of weeks after their arrival in Minnesota, Carl enrolled in a local university. Shortly after, he interviewed for and received a youth pastor position in the area.

But although Carl and Jenny praised God for his provision, they've now come to see that one of the main reasons for their return may have been something entirely beyond the surface circumstances of job and location. A few short weeks after their move to Minnesota, Jenny's father became sick, spiraling into a decline that continued until his death three years later.

"I had to deal with my bitterness that I had toward the situation and how it happened," Jenny said, especially regarding Carl's job loss. "God was like, 'I'm pruning you.' Even though there were things in our life that weren't bad, he was cutting them back so we could grow. But looking back on it, I remember thinking 'I'm so glad that we're in Minnesota because if we had been in Arizona we wouldn't have been there.' It was time with my dad that we wouldn't have had."

Looking back, it was that experience that helped her trust God when a similar situation arose years later.

"The second time—yes, it was still hurtful, but my anger and bitterness didn't last as long. I knew how to handle it," she said.

Despite having five children and no income, she again chose to rely on God.

"I still worry, but I don't stress out as much, because I know that something will work out—that God will take care of us, because that's what he does. He's proven that to us. You really have to trust him when you have nothing."

Conclusion

The stories of Naomi, Jarius, Julie, Kendra and Jenny reveal how our relationship with God precedes the ability to place our trust in his provision, especially in difficult circumstances. Just as we do not trust a complete stranger with our most precious possessions, our deepest feelings, or our greatest secrets, we cannot truly trust God without first establishing a relationship with him. God reveals himself in scripture, and we need to meet him there before we will truly hand him our fears, our desires, and our loved ones, trusting that he will meet us in times of great trial.

Prayer

Lord, thank you that we can trust you in the midst of illness, lost jobs, death, physical danger, and our times of greatest uncertainty. Thank you that during your years walking the earth, you were born in a stable, and became a refugee in Egypt as your family fled Herod. As an adult, you suffered persecution, mocking, severe physical beating, the death of a friend in Lazarus, betrayal by a disciple and all of mankind, an unjust trial in the dead of night, and a brutal death on the cross. You have personally experienced the worst pain possible on earth—and you meet us there, not as an outsider, but as someone who wipes our tears in intimate understanding and with tender compassion. Continue to draw us into a closer relationship with you. Remind us to set aside time daily to meet with you, talk with you, and read scripture. Reveal yourself to us in the little things as we learn to trust you with the big things. Thank you that you intercede for us constantly before God in heaven and hold us closest during our most difficult trials. Amen.

Your Turn

Read Ruth 2:1–20.

1. *How often do you find yourself needing to feel "in control" of a situation? Have you experienced a time where you were able to let go of a situation or person and trust God? What was the outcome?*

_____

_____

_____

2. *How easy or difficult is it for you to trust God in your life? Is it easier in some areas more than others (for example, consider things like finances, relationships, children, work)? Explain.*

_____

_____

_____

3. *Have you experienced a time you trusted Jesus, as Jarius did, regardless of what people around you said?*

_____

_____

_____

4. *Isaiah 40:31 [NLT] declares, "But those who trust in the Lord will find new strength. They will soar high on wings like eagles. They will run and not grow weary. They will walk and not faint." This chapter portrays people and situations that depended on God for strength. Can you think of a time when this occurred in your own life?*

_____

_____

_____

4

Evident Faith

"I will do whatever you say," Ruth answered. So she went down to the threshing floor and did everything her mother-in-law told her to do.

—*Ruth 3:5–6 (NIV 1984)*

Although Naomi and her family left during a time of famine, they returned during a time of plenty. God's timing was perfect: The barley harvest had just begun, and with it, the opportunity for Naomi and Ruth to experience God's provision through the generosity of others.

And yet, despite Naomi's knowledge, it was Ruth the Moabitess who exhibited extraordinary faith through action in this story. She had the courage to believe in God's promises and took action before she could see that he was moving. It was Ruth who, in faith, left her homeland to follow her mother-in-law, even when the obvious, logical choice was to return to her family, her culture, and her gods.

It was Ruth who took the initiative and the risk when, in faith, she went to the fields to glean behind the harvesters. Ruth did not initially glean in the fields of Boaz. She did not know, in advance, that she would stumble into Boaz's fields nor did she know, in advance, that he would show her such mercy.

And it was Ruth who, in faith, followed Naomi's instruction when she sought Boaz's protection as a kinsman-redeemer. God met Ruth as she stepped out in faith.

God does that. He often asks us to step forward, believing that he will meet us before we can see him move. God required those who followed him to step forward in faith throughout the Bible, and he calls us to do the same. Hebrews 11:6 (MSG) states, "It's impossible to please God apart from faith. And why? Because anyone who wants to approach God must believe both that he exists and that he cares enough to respond to those who seek him." Both the Old and New Testaments are filled with stories of people stepping out in faith and believing God before they could see physical evidence of his presence in the situation.

Poor Noah. God told him to build an ark. It wasn't raining. In fact, it didn't even look like it was going to rain. From a human perspective, there was no rational reason to build an ark. Noah couldn't even build the ark in secret. The ark was approximately one and a half football fields long and took years to build. Everyone in his community mocked and ridiculed him. Noah and his ark were the talk of the town. Imagine what you would do if God asked you to step forward in faith with your entire community watching. Yet it was because Noah knew God and had the faith to step forward when asked that he was able to preserve his family. Although others may have thought his actions absurd, Hebrews 11:7 (MSG) commends him: "By faith, Noah built a ship in the middle of dry land. He was warned about something he couldn't see, and acted on what he was told. The result? His family was saved. His act of faith drew a sharp line between the evil of the unbelieving world and the rightness of the believing world. As a result, Noah became intimate with God." Did Noah have any idea how critically important his yes to God was? What of our own choices? Do we have any idea, in the moment, of how saying yes to God might alter our lives?

I (Julie) have a vivid memory of being confronted with the crossroads of saying yes to God or continuing forward with my desire to do the opposite. In the moment, it seemed like a small decision without any significant lasting impact. In hindsight, my decision determined whether or not I would have missed out on one of the greatest gifts God has ever given me: meeting my husband, Aaron. I longed to have a boyfriend when I was in high school and college. But as much as I yearned for romance, I also happened to be afraid of any boy who showed the slightest interest in me. Anytime I thought a boy liked me romantically, or if I liked him, I immediately started avoiding him. I couldn't help it. I would get so tongue-tied and flustered that my physical reaction was to completely shut down and avoid him. My condition earned me the nickname "Avoidance Girl" from some of my college friends. It sounds funny, but in reality it was socially crippling. By the time I graduated from college, I had several platonic male friends, but I had gone on only two or three dates in my entire life and those dates had been awkward because I was intensely nervous. Honestly, I owe some very nice guys an apology for my behavior, which likely perplexed them.

I was twenty-one and in my first year of law school when I finally decided that I needed to overcome my fear of men. I figured the best thing to do was to simply jump into the dating game and go on lots of dates. Within a week of my new vow, I was a bridesmaid in a wedding. The bride and groom had secretly conspired to set me up with one of the groomsmen. He was a cute, sweet guy and I felt proud that I managed not to act nervous and freaky in his presence. As I drove home from the wedding that evening, I decided to send him an email. Even though I instinctively knew that he wasn't someone I wanted to marry, I rationalized that it was the perfect first step to getting over my fears. Immediately, the thought popped into my head that I needed to pray about whether or not I should contact this guy. *Okay,* I thought, *praying might be a good idea and certainly couldn't hurt.* I nonchalantly rattled off a brief prayer and then reached down to turn on the radio. Imagine my surprise when the lyrics to a popular song filtered through the speakers about a woman jumping in her car and driving away from a relationship without looking in the rearview mirror. I was stunned at the eerie coincidence. I turned off the car radio and prayed again. I told God that I didn't know whether he had just spoken to me through the song or not, but that I trusted him to work out my Avoidance Girl tendencies. I also told God that I would not pursue the groomsman. My longing for romance had not changed; I still longed for a boyfriend and a husband. But despite my desire, I decided to say yes to God and wait.

Two weeks later, I met the love of my life during class. He asked me to go on a walk, and we've been together since that first outing twelve years ago. As I look back now, I know that if I had emailed that other man, he would have said yes to a date with me and, two weeks later, I would have said no to my future husband's suggestion that we go on a walk. God asked me to wait because he knew Aaron was just around the corner. Sitting in my car, in that small window of time, I had no idea how important it was for me to say yes. My "yes" did not save the human race from an impending flood, but it saved me from guaranteed heartache and allowed me to be available when a godly man walked into my life.

Walk your Faith

Because faith is in a person's heart or soul, it is impossible for others to see it. The only way internal faith can be shown is through external actions or works. That is the point in James 2:18 (NIV): "But someone will say, 'You have faith; I have deeds.' Show me your faith without deeds, and I will show you my faith by my deeds." Actions are evidence of a vital, living faith in God. The only way internal faith can be revealed is through external action or works. We often use the phrase "actions speak louder than words" to convey the same concept. We cannot separate our faith in God from our actions. Whether or not we really have faith in God is revealed by how we react to the circumstances around us.

I (Kendra) had dreams of working with children. Having just finished a social work internship at the local elementary school, I felt fairly certain I would find a job in the same area after graduation. But as the months went on and no kid-related jobs became available, I began to look outside the scope of what I believed was my skill set. And like any recent graduate who needs to just start making money to pay back student loans, I began applying for any job that required a social work degree.

One résumé I sent was to the hospice program in my hometown. They were seeking a part-time social worker. Although I had sent out lots of applications to many different places, they were the only one who called back for an interview. I told myself that although it wasn't an area I knew much about, interviewing for the position would be a good way to practice for other interviews. Meanwhile, I had every intention of continuing to look for other jobs, since I knew I had no experience working with anyone other than children.

Imagine my surprise when I received a call from the supervisor offering me the position. Immediately, fear gripped my heart. I had no experience working with people who were dying, their families, or grief in general. I was a twenty-year-old woman who had tailored all of her school studies toward kids and working in a school. What did I know about this area of expertise? It was completely foreign to me. But before I could open my mouth to say no, the supervisor simply asked that I think about it for a few days and get back to her, which I agreed to do.

For the next two days I spent all my time thinking about how I should turn the job down, how it wasn't, *couldn't* be for me, how I wasn't equipped. But in the back of my mind, I had this nagging feeling that maybe this was something God wanted me to do, after all. One afternoon I sat in my room and finally sought his direction for my life. I laid out all my concerns, my worries that I wasn't right for the job and wasn't qualified, and my fears about stepping into the position. After I ranted to the Lord about my inadequacies, I waited for his response, sure he would agree with my reasoning.

But, as has so often been the case in my life, he did not. In fact, I felt him tell me that almost everything I had done in my life up to that point I could say I did on my own. Although I gave God credit for the blessings in my life, because he had gifted me to work with kids, it was well within my comfort zone. I felt the Lord telling me that he wanted me to take this job because it would be the first time in my life that I would need to rely fully on him for everything. And at the end of the day, when I did a good job, I would know—as he would—that my efforts were a result of him working through me. In that moment, I felt myself at a crossroads. I could continue to go down a path of what was comfortable and known to me or I could say yes to God and step out into the unknown. I chose the latter, and although I cannot say that the year I spent working with hospice was easy for me, I learned to trust God like never before. Did I do a wonderful job and become the best social worker that hospice program had known? Not even close. Sometimes, I barely made it through the day. But though there were many tears along the way, God used me despite my imperfections, and taught me about relying on him in a way I previously had not experienced.

In Matthew 8:8–14 (MSG), we find the story of a Roman centurion who believed God could and would move before he saw it happen. As Jesus was entering Capernaum, the soldier approached Jesus in a panic because his servant was sick and in terrible pain. Jesus responded by offering to go with the soldier to his house in order to heal the servant. "Oh no," the captain responded. "I don't want to put you to all that trouble. Just give the order and my servant will be fine." Jesus's reaction to the Roman's faith is one of genuine surprise. The Message uses the words "taken aback," the New International Version uses the word "amazed," and the King James Version uses the word "marveled" to describe Jesus's reaction. After all, Jesus encountered the centurion early in his ministry, before all twelve of his disciples have joined him. Amazed, Jesus declared that the Roman soldier had more simple trust than anyone he had met among God's chosen people, the Israelites, the people who grew up knowing and worshipping God. Jesus tells the soldier, "Go. What you believed could happen has happened." (Matthew 8:14 [MSG]) And with those words, we are told the servant was immediately healed.

What is it about the centurion that allowed his simple faith in Jesus to cause Jesus to be taken aback, amazed, and marvel? How is it that this man, a foreigner, was able to have more faith in God than the Israelites, the very people who were supposed to know about God and how he works? During his conversation with Jesus, the centurion explains, "Just give the order and my servant will be fine. I'm a man who takes orders and gives orders. I tell one soldier, 'go,' and he goes; to another, 'Come,' and he comes; to my slave, 'Do this,' and he does it." The centurion was accustomed to giving orders and having those orders obeyed as an officer in the Roman army and as a slave owner. He had faith in Jesus' ability to heal from afar based, in part, on his own experience commanding others. Although the centurion's personal experience gave him a unique perspective in believing in Jesus' ability, he still had to apply that knowledge when confronted with Jesus' offer to accompany him to his home. He still had to actively choose to exercise faith.

With more access than ever before to numerous translations of the Bible, we have an even greater advantage than Noah, Ruth, and the centurion had when it comes to exercising our faith. God reveals himself through scripture, so when we fill our hearts and our minds with God's Word, we learn his laws and promises. When we read the testimonies of people like Noah, Ruth, and the centurion, our own faith is bolstered. It is by reading scripture that we strengthen our relationship with God so that we have the faith and ability to say yes in the midst of a situation—even when we would rather say no.

Christa's Story

The emotional affair caught Christa off guard.

After all, she'd known her husband Jason most of her life. They'd attended the same grade school, gone to the same church, and had the same group of friends when they started dating the summer before her senior year of high school.

Over the years, they had built a good life together. They loved spending time outdoors together biking, hiking, and camping. After college, his proposal mirrored the lyrics to a country song, with the words "Will you marry me? Check Yes or No" inscribed on the note in the ring box. They started building a home together during their engagement, and moved in after returning from their honeymoon.

But by the time they had two small toddlers at home, life had become monotonous. Jason spent long hours working, while Christa adjusted to staying home full-time.

"Everything was fine. …Not really, really good, not really, really bad—just 'fine,'" Christa said. "And I think I needed to hear more from him about how he felt about me or recognizing how I was being as a mother. I'm sure I could have reciprocated that back at him too."

So when someone she saw from time to time started making personal comments to her, she felt conflicted. She knew that the comments were inappropriate to make to another man's wife, but mixed in with the guilt was pleasure. It felt good to be appreciated.

Her lack of communication with Jason was a huge factor, she said. Work was busy. And with two young children to chase after, their activities as a couple had tapered off.

"We weren't nurturing our marriage—we'd kind of lost that. Any energy went into the kids," she said.

When the comments and phone calls began, she was caught off guard. And yet, she started to think thoughts she hadn't thought before. She started losing interest in her marriage.

"All of this thought and energy was being put into this other person," she said. "Every time he'd see me, he'd say something nice to me and I loved hearing that."

Like her relationship with Jason, her relationship with God was struggling, too. They weren't consistently going to church at the time, although they had started the process of searching for one to attend. Both she and Jason were at a crossroads in their faith.

"At the time, I felt very disconnected to God. I wanted to be closer to him, but I knew I couldn't be because I had this major sin going on in my life," she said.

Although Jason knew something was wrong, Christa agonized over telling him the truth, finding it hard to verbalize how someone else was filling an emotional gap her husband hadn't realized was missing.

Finally, she confessed her situation to Jason. He was hurt, angry, and sad but, as time went on, proved to be loving, patient, and accepting of her struggles. They began to take action steps to revitalize their marriage.

"We sat down, and I said, 'I want to be married to you, but I need you to help me to want you. I love you, I do—but we need to work together,'" she said.

Telling Jason also helped break the secret's power in her life.

"I had more strength to not answer that phone call, or say, 'no, do not call me,'" she said. She stopped taking his calls; she changed her number.

Being accountable to her husband was freeing, she said. With freedom came the determination to be intentional in her relationships with her husband and with the Lord.

"Once I became right with Jason and took the action to say 'okay, this is going to stop,' then I was able to cry out to God, because I knew I could wholeheartedly," she said. "Numerous times throughout the day I would say, 'Put a desire in my heart for my husband. Put a desire in my heart for him. Change my heart.' All the time I would say it."

Within a couple of months, Christa felt changed, and her prayers changed, too. Instead of simply calling out to God, she began thanking him, praising him. She posted Psalm 26:3 (NIV 1984)—"For your love is ever before me and I walk continually in your truth"—on her bathroom mirror as a daily reminder to actively live out her faith.

"If I focused on his love, the love he had for me and me for him, I knew the other things would fall into place," she said.

Their relationship now is amazing, she said, marveling at how God turned a situation that was meant for their destruction into something that made them a better, stronger couple.

"It's nothing short of a miracle," she said. "Yeah, we have our struggles, but we know what to do now…so that it never goes that direction again because we know that this where God wants us to be, this is what he intended."

Now, Christa said, her love for her husband mirrors her love for the Lord.

"I'm a totally different person. I'm a new woman; I'm a new creation in Christ. I'm completely changed," she said. "It drew me to God, and at the same time, it drew me to my husband. Which I think is how God intended it to be."

Conclusion

Walking in faith isn't easy, just ask Ruth, Noah, the centurion and Christa. Christa's daily, sometimes hourly, reliance on God to help her rebuild her emotional bond with her husband helps illustrate how our faith is an active decision. After all, her marriage would not have been restored without her conscious decision to cut off all contact with the other man and firm commitment to dedicate her thoughts and emotions to God whenever they began to stray. Christa acted in faith, asking God to step in and turn her heart back to her husband *before* she could even feel renewed love and passion for Jason. In return, God was faithful to meet Christa in that hard place of believing his promises before her heart felt that answered prayer.

As women, how often do we allow our emotions to lead the way in our lives without pausing to seek God's will first? Our culture is permeated with the lie that our "hearts" (emotions) will somehow guide us toward perfect happiness. We use emotions to justify our decision to avoid those hard forks in the road between God's Word and our desires. Isn't the decision to follow our heart—even when we know it goes against God's Word—the very essence of selfishness? How many times has rashly following our hearts resulted in nothing but brokenness, bitterness, and regret? When we trust God enough to seek and follow his will, even when it conflicts with our momentary desire, he is good and faithful. God grows our character in those hard places and, when we are obedient despite our emotions, he often answers our prayers in ways that are beautifully beyond our hopes, dreams, and wildest expectations!

Prayer

Lord, remind us to turn to your Word instead of our hearts when we are faced at the crossroads of a decision. Like Christa, help us to set aside emotional desires when we know your response is the opposite and give us the strength and courage to step forward in faith before our heart follows, knowing you can and will change our heart's desire to mirror your own. If there is an area in our heart or life that does not line up with your Word, quietly reveal that area to us now. Give each of us a defining "line in the sand" moment in which we stop following our hearts and start following your will and your Word in that area. Give each of us courage, strength, and encouragement as we stand in faith on your words even when it is hard, even when it seems impossible, even when the world would tell us that things will never change. In those moments, remind us of Noah. Remind us of Ruth. Remind us of the centurion. And, remind us of Christa. Nothing, Lord, is impossible for you. You make the impossible, possible. You make the possible, reality. For those of us currently on the path of walking in faith, waiting for our hearts to catch up, speak to us through scripture. Encourage us on those difficult mornings when our hearts are screaming out to run in the opposite direction. Help us to hold tight to your Word while we wait. Remind us of your promises in scripture. Remind us of the countless others in the Bible and in our lives who walked in faith, ignored their hearts, and were blessed beyond their wildest dreams with the results. Line up our hearts, minds, emotions, and desires so they are in step with your Word, that we would not fight against you but would run with you in this race called life. Amen.

Your Turn

Read Ruth 2:21–3:6.

1. *Have you ever found yourself at a crossroads where God asked you to take a step of faith? What was the outcome?*

_____

_____

_____

2. *Hebrews 11:7 [MSG] states, "By faith, Noah built a ship in the middle of dry land. He was warned about something he couldn't see, and acted on what he was told. The result? His family was saved. His act of faith drew a sharp line between the evil of the unbelieving world and the rightness of the believing world. As a result, Noah became intimate with God."*

   a. *Have you ever taken a step of faith that may not have made sense at the time, but looking back, you can see was the right thing to do?*

_____

_____

_____

b. Noah became intimate with God as a result of his act of faith. In what ways have you seen your relationship with the Lord strengthened as a result of stepping out in faith?

_____

_____

_____

3. Like Christa, have you ever found yourself in a situation where your emotions differed from what you knew you should do? How did you respond and what was the result?

_____

_____

_____

4. "Actions are evidence of a vital, living faith in God. The only way internal faith can be revealed is through external action or works." This phrase implies that faith is not a one-time announcement or event, it is ongoing. What, even now, may God be asking you to do that would once again be a step of faith in your life?

_____

_____

_____

5. *How can remembering how God has met you in the past help you now to respond in faith?*

_____

_____

_____

5

True Sacrifice

"Yes, I know," Boaz replied. "But I also know about everything you have done for your mother-in-law since the death of your husband. I have heard how you left your father and mother and your own land to live here among complete strangers. May the Lord, the God of Israel, under whose wings you have come to take refuge, reward you fully for what you have done."

—*Ruth 2:11–12 (NLT)*

*R*uth knew the meaning of the word "sacrifice." She chose to follow her mother-in-law Naomi to a land and people not her own, even when given the option of turning back. Although her sister-in-law opted to return to her homeland, Ruth decided to stay. She chose the road of uncertainty, proclaiming allegiance to Naomi in such strong terms that her words are used in many marriage ceremonies today with the promise, "Your people will be my people, and your God my God." (Ruth 1:16 NLT) Culturally, Ruth was a Moabite, part of a group of people who were considered to be enemies of Israel, so her proclamation was a radical departure from what would be expected of her. The Old Testament is peppered with descriptions of wars and conflicts with the land of Moab. These were not peaceably neighboring countries, although they may have been in a period of peace during this story. So while Naomi was returning to her homeland in the journey back to Judah, Ruth was sacrificing everything she knew in terms of culture, comfort, and acceptance as she followed Naomi to Judah. Yet Ruth trusted Naomi, God, and Boaz, and took action steps based on that trust. Ultimately, she was rewarded for her trust: Boaz commended Ruth for leaving everything she knew and returning with Naomi, then spoke a blessing over her life. Her actions did not go unnoticed by Boaz or by God. God honors true sacrifice. And this sacrifice was the first step in what would ultimately become Ruth's redemption.

There are roughly 417 times that sacrifice is addressed in the Bible. In the Old Testament, the word "sacrifice" is mainly given in the context of animal sacrifice ritually performed as a way to honor God, offer thanksgiving, atone for sin, worship, and offer the first fruits. The New Testament moves beyond the sacrifice of many to the sacrifice of one—the sacrifice of a holy, sinless Jesus Christ. Romans 8:3 (NLT) states, "The law of Moses was unable to save us because of the weakness of our sinful nature. So God did what the law could not do. He sent his own Son in a body like the bodies we sinners have. And in that body God declared an end to sin's control over us by giving his Son as a sacrifice for our sins." God the Father loved us enough to send his son to die and Jesus became a willing sacrifice for our sins. He wasn't forced; he chose to lay his life down, breaking the hold that sin had on our lives. As he tells his disciples in the story written in Luke 22:20 (NLT), "After supper [Jesus] took another cup of wine and said, 'This cup is the new covenant between God and his people—an agreement confirmed with my blood, which is poured out as a sacrifice for you.'" Jesus's sacrifice established a new covenant between God and his people, offering grace like we had never known before. No longer did we need to offer animal sacrifices; the veil that separated man and God was torn in two. We now have free access to God, an invitation to a close personal relationship through Jesus. Although Christ's sacrifice altered our relationship with him, he still desires for us to offer sacrifices to him.

The question we face today is what does sacrifice look like for me, specifically? We may know of friends or family members who have chosen to give up things we have no desire to surrender, things which we've received no prompting from God to give up ourselves, and yet we wonder, *should I?* Or we've all heard amazing testimonies from people who have left everything to become a missionary in a foreign country, and although it sounds amazing, there may be part of us that thinks, *Lord, I'll do anything, just don't send me to Africa!* Or maybe you are the person who would love to be called to Africa and dread the idea of spending your life in familiar surroundings. Although the type of sacrifice may be unique to each of us, the Bible does lay out specific ways that all our lives should be a sacrifice before the Lord. Mark 12:33 (NLT) states, "And I know it is important to love him with all my heart and all my understanding and all my strength, and to love my neighbor as myself. This is more important than to offer all of the burnt offerings and sacrifices required in the law." Our sacrifices, then, should flow out of two motivations: our love for God and our care of others.

Love God

The first way that God asks us to offer our life as a sacrifice is to love him first and most. When a religious leader asked Jesus which commandment was most important, he emphasized, "The most important commandment is this... 'And you must love the Lord your God with all your heart, all your soul, all your mind, and all your strength.' The second is equally important: 'Love your neighbor as yourself.' No other commandment is greater than these." (Mark 12:29-31 [NLT])

God is not interested in what we can bring him or do for him if we do not love him. It's important to not just love him when it's convenient or when we are in a hard situation; he calls us to love him beyond anything or anyone else in our lives, to radically love him with a sacrificial kind of love. In Luke 14:26 (NLT) Jesus claims, "If you want to be my disciple, you must hate everyone else by comparison—your father and mother, wife and children, brothers and sisters—yes, even your own life. Otherwise, you cannot be my disciple." This is a hard scripture to read, and honestly, it makes us cringe a bit. We think, *How could I ever live up to that?* But I think the point God makes is that our love for him must trump everything else in life, big or small. He needs to come first. Every decision you and I make should have God's will and purpose in mind. My obedience to him must be in everything I do, not just from a sense of duty but because of my honest desire to love God first and most in my life.

I (Kendra) attended a Christian conference where the theme of the night was to "Be the Change." I was so excited to be at the conference because of the theme and all that I had felt God doing over the previous year that, at the beginning of the evening meeting, while the emcee made announcements and shared about the single moms' conference that would be coming up in the next month, I was happy to simply browse through my conference brochure, eager to read about all the upcoming sessions and speakers. Despite my inattention, I listened with half an ear as the emcee explained how they would be having a shop for the single moms to get a new outfit for free at the conference. She concluded, "So if anyone has bought something new that they'd be willing to donate to bless a single mom, we're taking donations tonight and in the morning." Immediately, I thought of the new yellow shirt I had purchased that afternoon while out shopping with my friends. I quickly disregarded the thought, telling myself how excited I was to wear it the next day. After the announcements, the main speaker got up and spoke about her experience living as a missionary in Africa with her husband. She told amazing stories of how God had literally saved their lives on many occasions. During her talk, I thought about all the great things God had called my husband and I to do in the past year: being part of a church plant, joining the speaking team, and directing the community groups. They all felt like big steps of faith to me and as I reflected on them, I was so thankful for all that God had done in and through us in the process.

At the close of the service, while we were again worshiping God and I praised him for who he was and all that he'd done in my life, the emcee came up to close the service. She again reminded us to bring any new items the next day to bless single moms who needed it. Again, my yellow shirt came to mind, but I told myself, *Oh, that's such a small thing, it won't really matter with all the big ways I've stepped out in faith this past year.* The words had just formed in my mind when I felt a voice ask, *But can you obey me in the small things?* Immediately, I knew it was God speaking. I also knew I would need to donate my new purchase the next day. I quickly asked the Lord's forgiveness. As we walked out of the conference, I told my friends what had happened, and they agreed that I needed to give my shirt away. The next day, I brought my beautiful new yellow shirt and gave it to a young woman collecting donations. She gladly thanked me for the donation and told me it would make some mom very happy.

As I turned around, I began to cry. It's funny how something so simple can at times feel like such a sacrifice. I realized in that moment that I had almost missed an opportunity to be obedient to God, and I shuddered to think I would disregard his voice so easily. I left the conference fully renewed to listen to and obey God in both the big and small things.

Take Care of Others

It doesn't matter who we are: If we call ourselves Christians, we are called to care for others. Hebrews 13:16 (NLT) tells believers, "And don't forget to do good and to share with those in need. These are the sacrifices that please God." Whether that takes the form of helping family members or an elderly neighbor, volunteering at a battered women's shelter, or simply caring for those at our workplace, we are all called by God to see beyond ourselves and consider the needs of others. In fact, God's desire that we would help others out of a sacrificial heart is more than just a suggestion—it's a command:

> *No, this is the kind of fasting I want: Free those who are wrongly imprisoned; lighten the burden of those who work for you. Let the oppressed go free, and remove the chains that bind people. Share your food with the hungry, and give shelter to the homeless. Give clothes to those who need them, and do not hide from relatives who need your help.* (Isaiah 58:6–7 [NLT])

I (Julie) recently listened to the stories of a man who intentionally lived as a homeless person for five months. He spoke of people— even those who claimed to be Christians—deliberately becoming preoccupied with their phones, their conversations, or the world around them as they walked past him so they would not have to meet his eyes. He and his companions felt like the constant, intentional avoidance of eye contact robbed them of their humanity. Out of all of the things they experienced, it was this deliberate dismissal of their very existence that left lasting scars. So often, I have fiddled with the knobs on my car's radio so that I could avoid the gaze of the man standing at the intersection. I have suddenly become very interested in the contents of my purse, the color of the sky, or the scuffs on my shoes so that I might walk by without having to acknowledge the human sitting on the sidewalk five feet away. As I heard this speaker describe his experience at the hands of professed Christians, my heart broke. In the biblical account of the Good Samaritan, I was the priest and the Levite who passed by instead of stopping to help. I'd always thought of myself somewhat smugly as a "good" person who helped others. As this man spoke, I realized that I stop to help people who are clean, dressed nicely, and smell pretty. How did I forget all of the dirty, smelly, or otherwise inconvenient people I have passed by and pretended not to notice? That realization was like a punch in the gut. The great thing about God is that he so often gives us second chances. I confessed my sin that night and vowed that I would never again intentionally avoid the eyes of a homeless person. I promised myself I would put some supplies in my purse so that I would have a little something to give to anyone I might meet on the street.

One week later, as I was driving home, I saw him. He was a very young man, grubby, wearing a backpack and holding a sign at the intersection. It was a red light. My heart started pounding; this was the test of my vow. While everyone in the cars around me fiddled with the knobs on their radios, I started frantically searching through my car for something to share. As I mentally berated myself for not yet stashing anything in my purse, I found a plastic bag full of snacks for my two young children. I grabbed the bag full of assorted animal crackers, fruit snacks, and Cheerios, rolled down my window and began waving the bag and shouting to the young man. I'm certain I did not say anything brilliant in those twenty seconds of conversation, and I'm not sure what he thought of the bag of toddler snacks I left with him, but I gazed deeply into his eyes while we spoke. I don't know if that experience changed him, but I know it changed me. I now have a stash of supplies in my car. I take five minutes out of my busy day to dart across intersections with a small token in my hands so that I might meet the eyes of a stranger. I am not foolish enough to think that my new hobby changes anyone's life dramatically, but being obedient to God by taking a moment out of a busy day to acknowledge someone's existence has changed my life.

Why is sacrifice so important to God? Because it takes the focus off of us and places it firmly on God and others. It gives us the opportunity to be obedient to him in a way we would not otherwise be able to be, and this pleases God. Second Corinthians 2:15 (NLT) says, "Our lives are a Christ-like fragrance rising up to God." We are never more fragrant than when we are willing to say yes to God and show others his love.

This kind of sacrifice can be scary, and the thought that we could get hurt or taken advantage of by others is a very real possibility. The idea of leaving people I love or giving up things I enjoy or am familiar with is hard. But that is exactly what God asks of us; he wants anything removed that would try to take his place. Just the other day, I (Kendra) was thinking about how much I love the ten-year-old boy we are in the process of adopting, but I found myself becoming jealous. Although he loves us, he doesn't call us mom and dad, and he is still very attached to his birth mother. I cried out to God, wondering, "Will he ever know how much we love him? Will he know we have, and will, sacrificed for him, that we see him as our child? How long do you love someone without ever knowing if they'll love you back? Who *does* that?" Immediately I was struck by the realization: God does that. He loved us while we were sinners, with no promise that we would love him back. And in fact, many people never love him. Even those of us who are Christians can find ourselves loving other people or things more than God. As I sat, brokenhearted, I had a new sense to always choose God first in my life. And I took comfort in knowing that he knows my heart, my struggles, and my feelings for my son.

Carol's Story

For Pastor Carol, the flashing lights in her rearview mirror on a Tuesday night were the proverbial icing on the cake.

It had already been a tough week. Her son had gotten married the previous Saturday, so she was out of the office Friday and home, exhausted, on Monday. And then her dad's surgery ran two hours late on Tuesday, which pushed back everything else, including a speaking engagement at a local church's women's event that evening.

As cofounders and pastors at Place of Hope Ministries, Carol and her husband, Geary, help provide both immediate shelter and permanent housing to those experiencing homelessness, meals for the hungry, kid-focused outreach, a discipleship program, jail and prison outreach, church services, and other ministries, among other things.

Getting pulled over may not have been in her original plan—she almost missed the turnoff to the church and got pulled over for skipping the turn lane—but finally rushing inside the church and seeing a table full of Place of Hope women she had mentored and seen life changes in made it all worthwhile.

"I just felt like 'I don't even need to talk, because they speak for themselves,'" she said. "We don't need to say anything: Just look and see what the Lord has done."

We Are Alive

It's taken a long time to get to this point. Carol grew up on a farm in a small town and started doing alcohol and drugs at twelve. Although she tried to stop several times on her own, it wasn't until she and her husband became Christians in 1980 that she was finally able to quit.

For Carol, the change was immediate.

"It's hard for me to understand people who get saved and nothing changes," she said. "I just don't get it, because we went from black to white—we went from 'we are dead, to we are alive.' My whole life changed."

Geary got his pastoral license in 1988, and after being a stay-at-home mom to their three children for twelve years, Carol decided to get her pastoral license as well. After obtaining an additional degree in chemical dependency and psychology, an internship at Minnesota Teen Challenge segued into getting hired as program director.

But even while working there, she and her husband began to feel a call to go elsewhere.

"I felt the Lord really spoke to me that we were going to have a facility that helped families—men, women, and families—in addiction and poverty," she said. "And then in 1996, the Lord spoke to us about St. Cloud."

She and her husband founded Place of Hope Ministries in St. Cloud in 1997.

He Shall Sustain You

Over the years, Psalm 55:22 (New King James Version) has become Carol's favorite verse: "Cast your burden on the Lord and he shall sustain you."

"Because I play piano, that means a lot," she said. "The word sustain means 'to hold,' and if you hit a note on the piano, you push the sustain pedal and it holds it. When I was first saved, the Lord gave me that verse."

As a new Christian, Carol held on to that verse through the financial crises that followed.

"I remember when I first got saved, reading the little pamphlet that said, 'God has a wonderful plan for your life.' And in my head, that meant a big, beautiful house. He had a wonderful plan, all right, but that wasn't it," she said, chuckling.

Before they were Christians, her husband always had a job, and since they lived within their means, they never worried about money.

"The minute we got saved, it's like all hell broke loose in our life," she said. Within four months of uprooting everything to move to a new town, Geary lost his job. With three kids and no money in the midst of the economically depressed 1980s, it was a bad situation. But Geary insisted that God would provide.

One day, the Lord told Carol to make a grocery list and place it on her windowsill.

"I put the list on the window, and we just prayed," she said. A day later, a woman Carol had never met—someone who had heard about them from a mutual acquaintance—showed up with a carload of groceries.

"I was blown away. I'd never experienced anything like that," she said. "She left, and as I began to unload them, I got to the two cans of Chicken of the Sea tuna and I *knew*—I went into shock, and I went and got my list—*everything* that was on there was in these bags. We didn't even know what we were doing, and God was faithful to us."

Those early years were a training ground for Carol's challenges today.

"Because of that, we can run Place of Hope. Because every day, it's the same. Every day, I'm making my list. *Okay, Lord, is this what I need today?* And he routinely comes through, usually at the last minute," she said. "I would love it if we could pull from a big fund. But we don't, we have to pull from the Lord. He's our provider."

Early in their ministry, the Lord told her that her ministry would be like George Mueller, who ran an orphanage.

"He prayed everything in, to the point that trucks would break down in front of their place, full of milk or whatever else, and they would get it all," she said. "That's what happens to us all the time. I've had them call—'I've got a semi over here, their refrigeration unit's going out, and we've got to get rid of all of this'—or they'll pull in our yard and say, 'Somebody told me to come to Place of Hope with this stuff.' It's a miracle. We run a ministry based on miracles every day. So that's why I can't take any credit for it because God is doing it. And he's doing it because he loves people."

Over the years, being true to the call has meant a number of sacrifices. Just before starting Place of Hope and within the first year of its inception, Carol was offered two well-paying jobs. But even though they were good opportunities, they were a distraction from what they knew they were called to do.

Several years later, Carol was called to make another big sacrifice. After years of having a drop-in site in one area of town, they bought a 57,000-square-foot building to expand their services.

"I actually lived there for two years," Carol said. "It was very difficult. We had no staff, and we had a giant 57,000-square-foot building that was a miracle to get. And so I lived there. I was the men's staff, the women's staff, the custodian—I had to stay on site twenty-four hours a day. It was craziness."

Looking at the big picture, though, the momentary sacrifice was worth it.

"Some people can only see where they're at, and they can't see where they're going. In order to do anything for the Lord, you really have to see where you're going so you understand the sacrifice in the moment," she said. "There might be a sacrifice right now but you know what, it will pay later. Maybe not pay to you, but it will pay. I did live there for two years; it was very difficult. But it was a necessary thing that had to happen in order for us to build to where we could be, and now, we're at a point where we still sacrifice and we still give but we're teaching other people to be sacrificial but to keep their boundaries, especially with their families."

Investing in Others

Even though she's no longer there twenty-four hours a day, Carol still wears so many hats that she jokingly says she's going for the "layered look." In the past two years, they have continued to expand, building an apartment complex and landing contracts with the local Veterans Affairs Medical Center and Department of Corrections.

But she and her husband have gotten to the point where they are looking to the future, intentionally training and delegating to others. Part of that mentorship is teaching others how to give sacrificially.

"Right now we're at a point where people are learning to sacrifice—not sacrifice their families or their minds—but sacrificial giving for God," she said. "Our whole call is Isaiah 58, which talks about the 'true fast'—not just going without food, but actually doing things for the Lord instead of talking about it. And then it says that you will be called to rebuild, repair and restore streets. That's what our whole ministry's focused on that and that's what sustains me. The call sustains me."

At one point early in her ministry when she felt discouraged, a friend told her to remember that "you don't have a cause, you have a call."

"I thought, absolutely. I don't have a cause, I'm not out fighting for something, I have a call. I don't have to fight for my call, I have it. Now I just need to do what God's called me to do," she said.

That extends to their relationships with others, as well.

"We try to surround ourselves with people who have vision," she said. "I want people who know that they can do a piece of the ministry, but they have to see the big picture…That's my heart. I love to teach people to accept their gifts and their callings and understand what God has for them and not try to be somebody else, but be who God's called you to be."

Conclusion

Although the sacrifices we make now may sometimes hurt, scare us, or have others questioning our sanity, the payoff can be huge. Just as Ruth could not have known what was in store for her when she chose to travel with Naomi, and Carol could have never known how the ministry God called her to so many years ago would grow to where it is today, you may not be able to see everything God has in store for you. Ask yourself: Do I trust

God? Do I believe that his plans for my life are good no matter how things look right now?

In the New Testament, Jesus echoes Boaz's commendation of Ruth and expands on it to include all believers by stating, "I assure you, everyone who has given up house or wife or brothers or parents or children, for the sake of the Kingdom of God, will be repaid many times over in this life, as well as receiving eternal life in the world to come." (Luke 18:29–30 [NLT]) Our lives are not so different from the lives of Ruth, Naomi, or Carol. Although our sacrifice might look different from theirs, we are all called at one time or another to give up something, to put God first, and to love him most. The choice on whether or not we will choose to obey, however, is up to us.

Prayer

Lord, speak to each of us individually about what our lives should look like, without comparing ourselves to those around us. Grant us wisdom as we seek your will for our lives. Give us the courage to say yes to you, to step beyond our comfort zones, and to trust you to meet us as we step out in faith. Help us to say yes even when the path is not what we envisioned, even when we don't know how you will work out the details, even when we have to rely upon your provision instead of our own. Thank you that your plans for us are good—and that saying yes to you is ultimately always better than anything we would have planned for our own lives. Amen.

Your Turn

Read Ruth 2:11–12.

1. *What, if anything, in your life have you sacrificed for the Lord?
   What was the outcome?*

_____

_____

_____

2. *Is there something, even now, that the Lord is asking you to
   sacrifice?*

_____

_____

_____

3. *Have you ever been ridiculed or put down for your sacrificial giving? What encouragement do you receive from stories
   of women who sacrificed extravagantly for God, as Ruth and
   Carol have done?*

_____

_____

_____

4. How is God speaking to you to care for others in a way you may or may not already be doing?

_____

_____

_____

5. In Matthew 19:29 [NLT], it states, "And everyone who has given up houses or brothers or sisters or father or mother or children or property, for my sake, will receive a hundred times as much in return and will inherit eternal life." What encouragement do you receive from this passage that will help you to start or continue to live a life of sacrifice?

_____

_____

_____

Answered Prayer

"I am your servant Ruth," she said. "Spread the corner of your garment over me, since you are a kinsman-redeemer."

—*Ruth: 3:9 (NIV 1984)*

Tracing our ancestry and lineage has become easier as old, even ancient, records have become digitized and placed online in searchable databases. For most of us in the United States, researching our lineage is simply an enjoyable pastime rather than a necessity. That was not the case for the Israelites in the time of Ruth and Naomi. Ancestry was *the* defining criteria for the Israelites. The Israelites were the chosen people of God because of their heritage as the twelve tribes of Judah, descended directly from Abraham and Sarah. Jews today still find their identity primarily through birth to a Jewish mother (or parent) and secondarily through conversion to Judaism.

Ancestry was an important concept in the Israelite culture, and it's one of the reasons the cultural concept of the levirate marriage was considered necessary. In the event that an Israelite woman was widowed without children, the laws of the levirate marriage could be invoked. A brother or close relative (kinsman) was expected to marry the widow of his childless, deceased brother. The firstborn child born in that new marriage was treated as the child and heir of the deceased brother rather than the biological father (Gen. 38:8; Deut. 25:5–6). Although this sounds weird and unnatural to those of us living in free societies where women have the same rights and opportunities as their male counterparts, the levirate marriage laws were critical to protecting women in patriarchal societies in which they were otherwise often unable to provide for themselves. These laws were part of the social safety net of that culture.

With that perspective in mind, let's reconsider Naomi. She had two married sons, and it seems likely that she eagerly awaited grandchildren and, specifically, grandsons. In her society, Naomi's legacy was found in grandsons. Grandsons were the promise of the next generation, the continuation of her family line, her identity, and her legacy. Naomi "counted" because she was part of a family line that could (and would) be tracked and recounted hundreds of years into the future through the names of her sons and grandsons. When Naomi's husband and two sons died, not only was she left to face an uncertain future for her immediate survival, but she also lost her legacy. The family line was dead. There would be no sons or grandsons to carry on the line of Elimach, her husband. Naomi was probably too old to remarry and bear more children. She went from being a blessed woman among women to being pitied, a woman unsupported, worthless, and without the time or youth to redeem her legacy.

It is one thing to consider the Naomi who lived thousands of years ago and breeze quickly over the enormity of her situation; it is quite another to consider Naomi's plight in modern terms and then place ourselves in her shoes. How would we respond if our career was suddenly stripped from us? What if our husband or children turned their backs on us in undeserved rejection? What if our possessions were seized? What if we, without warning and without fault, were suddenly faced with a past stripped of any value, facing a future without enough time to recreate a life or a legacy? That was Naomi. Would we have the courage and strength to respond in faith in the midst of personal devastation, as she did? Yet it is Naomi's knowledge of God and his law regarding levirate marriage that, when acted upon, is a step toward redemption for both Ruth and Naomi:

> *One day her mother-in-law Naomi said to Ruth, "My dear daughter, isn't it about time I arranged a good home for you so you can have a happy life? And isn't Boaz our close relative, the one with whose young women you've been working? Maybe it's time to make our move. Tonight is the night of Boaz's barley harvest at the threshing floor. Take a bath. Put on some perfume. Get all dressed up and go to the threshing floor. But don't let him know you're there until the party is well under way and he's had plenty of food and drink. When you see him slipping off to sleep, watch where he lies down and then go there. Lie at his feet to let him know that you are available to him for marriage. Then wait and see what he says. He'll tell you what to do. Ruth said "If you say so, I'll do it, just as you've told me."* (Ruth 3:1–5 [MSG])

The scene at the threshing floor is festive. The barley harvest is in, and Boaz and his workers are celebrating the completion of their hard work. The story continues to unfold:

> *She went down to the threshing floor and put her mother-in-law's plans into action. Boaz had a good time, eating and drinking his fill—he felt great. Then he went off to get some sleep, lying down at the end of a stack of barley. Ruth quietly followed; she lay down to signal her availability in*

marriage. In the middle of the night the man was suddenly startled and sat up. Surprise! This woman asleep at his feet! He said, "And who are you?" She said, "I am Ruth, your maiden; take me under your protecting wing. You are my close relative, you know, in my circle of covenant redeemers—you do have the right to marry me." (Ruth 3:6–9 [MSG])

Although this may sound slightly scandalous, Ruth and Naomi's actions were completely appropriate and were within the custom and law of their day. Ruth prepared herself and dressed as she would have on her wedding day before she went to the threshing floor to sleep at Boaz's feet. Both Ruth and Boaz are described in the story as being godly, honorable individuals. Naomi would not have suggested such actions, Ruth would not have undertaken those actions, and Boaz would not have reacted as he did if they were behaving inappropriately.

But after Ruth's obedient journey to the threshing floor, the story makes a profound shift. Ruth and Naomi are no longer the central characters. The focus in the third chapter and entire fourth chapter of the book of Ruth is on the actions of other people, particularly a man named Boaz. It was Boaz who called together the town elders and the man with first right to be Ruth's kinsman-redeemer. It was Boaz who negotiated the cultural details so he and Ruth could marry. After Ruth obediently approached Boaz on the threshing floor, the implementation of the plan was left to Boaz. Ruth and Naomi were faithful to know God and his laws, and to act in faith on his promises. They were then asked to wait.

Giving and Receiving Assistance

The notion that Naomi and Ruth did not pull themselves out of their difficulties is a profound realization in our culture of deeply ingrained independence: "I can do it on my own, thank you very much." Unlike our modern idea of the mythical woman who wears her Wonder Woman undies under her street clothes, who has the perfect career, perfectly tidy house, perfectly mannered children (enrolled in six different activities at all times), the perfect body, and yet *still* manages to put a nutritious, gourmet dinner on the table each night that definitely did *not* come from a box, Naomi and Ruth reached a point in their journey where they needed someone to intervene, to take action in their lives, and to rescue them. God did not grant them the power to pull themselves out of their situation, although they were certainly no damsels in distress! Ruth and Naomi had to take affirmative steps toward God first, and *then* God, through Boaz, met them and carried the plan to completion.

When did we start believing the lie that we are able to do it all by ourselves without accepting, on occasion, the assistance from a fellow Christ follower? And on the flip side of the independence deception, do we say yes to God when we are nudged to go out of our way in order to meet a need for someone else? Or do we pass by, justifying our inaction by silently accusing that person of not helping him or herself?

God is clear on this topic: followers of Christ are to rely upon one another, work together, and pool their individual gifts and talents to be used collectively and cooperatively.

In chapter 12 of First Corinthians, Paul addresses the issue of different spiritual gifts given to followers of Christ. There must have been mutterings and comparisons about whose gifting was most important, most honorable, or most impressive because

Paul explains that "there are different kinds of spiritual gifts, but the same Spirit is the source of them all. There are different kinds of service, but we serve the same Lord. God works in different ways, but it is the same God who does the work in all of us. A spiritual gift is given to each of us so we can help each other." Paul continues with an analogy:

> *Yes, the body has many different parts, not just one part. If the foot says, "I am not a part of the body because I am not a hand," that does not make it any less a part of the body. And if the ear says, "I am not part of the body because I am not an eye," would that make it any less a part of the body? If the whole body were an eye, how would you hear? Or if your whole body were an ear, how would you smell anything? But our bodies have many parts, and God has put each part just where he wants it. How strange a body would be if it had only one part! Yes, there are many parts, but only one body. The eye can never say to the hand, "I don't need you." The head can't say to the feet, "I don't need you." In fact, some parts of the body that seem weakest and least important are actually the most necessary. And the parts we regard as less honorable are those we clothe with the greatest care. So we carefully protect those parts that should not be seen, while the more honorable parts do not require this special care. So God has put the body together such that extra honor and care are given to those parts that have less dignity. This makes for harmony among the members, so that all the members care for each other. If one part suffers, all the parts suffer with it, and if one part is honored, all the parts are glad. All of you together are Christ's body, and each of you is a part of it. (1 Cor. 12:14–27 [NLT])*

God asks us to hold out our hand in assistance to our brothers and sisters in Christ, not because he *needs* us, but because he *allows* us to experience the joy of helping someone else. There is something that changes in our heart when we extend a hand to help another. If we refuse God's nudging, he will sometimes find someone else who will say yes to complete the task first offered to us. He does not need you or me. Rather, he *invites* us to join him because he knows that when we say yes, our faith grows stronger and our relationship with him deepens. When we get to heaven, we will regret all the times we were invited to help another but declined because we were too busy shuttling kids to practice, cleaning house, watching TV, or spending an extra hour at work. As we intentionally start saying yes to God, despite being busy, God works out our schedules for us.

Take Lisa* for instance. Her experience is the perfect example of the profound impact a fellow Christian can have by being obedient to the nudging of God. Lisa had a difficult time talking to her dad about where he stood in his relationship with God. Although he would indulge her and listen as she prattled on about her church or Bible study, he held his own beliefs close. Not knowing whether their family's previous bad experience at a church had soured him on church, God, or both, Lisa struggled with how to raise the topic, whether or not it was her place to say anything, and how to begin the conversation. She loved her dad deeply, but struggled with whether or not she could relate to him and his experience. And so, Lisa prayed for her dad and for wisdom from God.

One day, her dad was drinking coffee in a small town café, catching up on recent happenings from the locals. As he was sipping his coffee, a stranger walked in, bought a cup of coffee, and sat next to Lisa's father. Out of the blue, he asked her dad whether he knew Jesus as his Lord and Savior. Rather than being put off by the stranger's question, Lisa's dad responded positively, sparking a deeply spiritual conversation. In the space of a morning, this stranger and Lisa's father had the heart-to-heart conversation that she did not know how to have with him. After their conversation, the stranger said his goodbyes and walked out of the café. Lisa has often thought of this man and his obedience to God's nudging to strike up that bold conversation that she herself was unable to have with her dad.

Remember that when we obey the nudging of the Lord to step out in faith to help a stranger, we are helping someone's child, parent, sibling, neighbor, or friend.

Accepting Help from Others

Just as we are sometimes the "rescuer," that also means that sometimes we are in the position of Ruth and Naomi, the "rescued." Sooner or later, we all face circumstances in our lives when we need a brother or sister in Christ to come alongside us.

I (Julie) was pregnant with my daughter when the sciatic nerve in my hip first started bothering me. I went on a day-long shopping excursion with my family when I was approximately five months pregnant and awoke the next day with unbelievable pain in my hip. Although it would improve at times, pain became my constant companion. My stride was tortured, my steps tentative as it felt like my leg would buckle each time weight was applied, and my sweet husband even had to help me with the humiliating task of putting on underwear, pants, and shoes in the mornings. It took me *minutes* to walk up steps. I couldn't step up on a curb, instead having to walk to a point where the curb was tapered to street level for wheelchair users. It was humiliating. Everyone could tell there was something seriously wrong with me the moment I tried to move. I prayed. I cried. My husband quietly and without complaint took on vacuuming and other chores I couldn't do. I felt like a failure of a wife. My doctor told me there was nothing to do but hope it was pregnancy-related pain.

And then, one day after more than two months of constant pain, it was gone. I rejoiced! I praised God and put the entire episode behind me as a big lesson learned in humility and in caring for others with a physical disability.

My condition reoccurred a year later without warning, during a time when I was not pregnant. No one could tell me what was medically wrong, whether it would ever go away, or if I could expect to walk normally again. As the months dragged by with no relief, I was referred to The Mayo Clinic to see a specialist. Although I prayed and tried to wait on God, I also secretly began to panic about what might be wrong with me. I wondered about cancer. I wondered whether I would ever run around outside with my kids. As I continually smiled and assured everyone around me that I was fine, that this was temporary, and that it would all be okay, I was eaten up inside with secret fears. There were many long nights in which my pillow was soaked in tears as I prayed to God.

During these long months, a friend continually suggested that I seek out the advice of his father, a retired Christian chiropractor. This man was in his seventies and had a small office in his house so he could continue practicing, simply because he loved helping others. After months of being offered his help, I finally set aside my pride and reluctance and agreed to go. After my first visit, I knew I made the correct choice. He saw my problem in terms of my entire body. He was not fooled by the symptoms in my hip; he looked for the root of the problem and adjusted my hips, back, and neck accordingly. This Christian man was my answered prayer. And, his repeated refusals to accept payment humbled me and reminded me of what it is to help others without expectation of receiving something in return. Over the course of a month and a few chiropractic adjustments, my body healed and my pain was gone. My ability to walk was fully restored.

Although I wish I could say that I was healed completely, I wasn't and haven't been. But, I've learned how to manage the flare-ups. And, as my condition has continued to reoccur, my prayers have shifted. I still pray for healing, but I've also begun praying that, while I wait for healing, the Lord would use my physical weakness and vulnerability as a way to reach others. My shifted prayers have opened the doors to amazing conversations.

Although I believe God can and sometimes does heal people in an immediate response to prayer, I also accept that he often answers prayers in unexpected ways and delays healing our physical bodies for a variety of reasons. God worked through another person to redeem my quality of life and gave me the insight on how to control future flare-ups. I did not have the knowledge to fix it myself, although I certainly tried. It took a soft-spoken, wise, sweet older gentleman who follows Christ to show me that the human body has to work in tandem together, and that when one neck vertebrae is misaligned, it just might show up in a crippled hip.

God often uses the hands and feet of other people to accomplish his will. Romans 12:4-5 (NLT) sums it up perfectly: "Just as our bodies have many parts and each part has a special function, so it is with Christ's body. We are many parts of one body, and we all belong to each other." Paul's exhortation to help fellow believers was a simple restatement of the broader example already set by Jesus Christ:

Just then a religion scholar stood up with a question to test Jesus. "Teacher, what do I need to do to get eternal life?" He answered, "What's written in God's Law? How do you interpret it?" He said, "That you love the Lord your God with all your passion and prayer and muscle and intelligence—and that you love your neighbor as well as you do yourself." "Good answer!" said Jesus. "Do it and you'll live." Looking for a loophole, he asked, "And just how would you define 'neighbor'?"

Jesus answered by telling a story. "There was once a man traveling from Jerusalem to Jericho. On the way he was attacked by robbers. They took his clothes, beat him up, and went off leaving him half-dead. Luckily, a priest was on his way down the same road, but when he saw him he angled across to the other side. Then a Levite religious man showed up; he also avoided the injured man.

"A Samaritan traveling the road came on him. When he saw the man's condition, his heart went out to him. He gave him first aid, disinfecting and bandaging his wounds. Then he lifted him onto his donkey, led him to an inn, and made him comfortable. In the morning he took out two silver coins and gave them to the innkeeper, saying, 'Take good care of him. If it costs any more, put it on my bill—I'll pay you on my way back.'

"What do you think? Which of the three became a neighbor to the man attacked by robbers?" "The one who treated him kindly," the religion scholar responded. Jesus said, "Go and do the same." (Luke 10:25–37 [MSG])

What isn't immediately clear from this story is the tension between the Jews and the group of people identified as Samaritans in that day and culture. Israelites and Samaritans did not get along. In fact, the Israelites despised the Samaritans. The story Jesus told in answer to the religious man's question about how to get to heaven revealed that the two so-called good, righteous, religious people (the priest and the Levite) failed when given the opportunity to put their faith into physical action. It was the Samaritan, a person disdained by many, who acted as a neighbor by stepping in to rescue the injured man.

Paul calls us to assist our fellow Christ followers. But Jesus calls us to assist everyone, even the unlovely and despicable.

Susan's Story

As Susan* left her husband after twelve years of marriage, his final vow rang in her ears: He would use all the money he had to take their three sons away from her.

A failed marriage was never something Susan had pictured. After meeting the seemingly charming Mark while finishing her degree and getting married soon after, it wasn't long before the dreams she had for her marriage quickly turned to the nightmarish reality of suffering under Mark's abusive tendencies.

"After leaving him early on in our marriage, I told him, if he ever physically hurt me again that I would leave," Susan said. "After an incident of attempted rape by him, I knew I had to follow through with my promise."

But the years of physical, emotional, verbal, and spiritual abuse had taken a toll. Terrified to follow through on her promise to leave Mark, Susan sought out counseling. Finally, as her fear of further abuse escalated, she summoned the courage to leave.

Her oldest son, Tim, cried. He didn't want to leave the farm they called home, so despite her desire to take him with her, she allowed him to remain with Mark, since his physical abuse had never extended to their children.

Mark's assault on Susan's relationship with her children began immediately. During their divorce proceedings, he threatened her life, forcing her to take out a restraining order against him.

"My now ex-husband never gave up blaming me for the divorce, and was very verbal about it with my boys," she said. He would tell her sons that the divorce was Susan's fault: she was the one who chose to leave the family; she broke up the marriage; and she was the one taking their money. "This caused my boys unbelievable pain and suffering."

Their acrimonious divorce took a toll on her sons, and for many years, it appeared that Mark's words would come true. Her oldest son, Tim, continued to live with his father. By the time he turned eleven, her middle son, Andy, began running away from home and was placed in foster care before being transferred to live with his father. And at the age of fourteen, Susan's youngest son, Jeremy, decided to move in with his father and brothers as well.

Though she tried to maintain contact with her sons, increasingly, Susan found her efforts rebuffed.

"I rarely saw my boys or spoke with them after they moved in with their dad," she said. "I would attempt to go to school conferences and sporting events to show them I loved them, but they would have nothing to do with me. My phone calls were futile, and always ended in angry words."

Desperate, Susan wondered if things would ever change. She felt guilt over her failed marriage, and blamed herself for what she saw as failing her children. Struggling with depression, she closed off her heart to others.

"My life was a nightmare, and I saw no end in sight," she said. "It was the most painful experience imaginable, having your children torn away from you. They saw me as the enemy."

A Time of Waiting

As the years went by with little to no change, Susan began to cry out to God. She became more diligent about reading her Bible and praying. But still she struggled.

"I often wondered if the Lord heard my cries for help and if my life would ever be different," Susan said. "Many times I had to surrender control of my boys and my situation and give it over completely to him. I cried out to him often, wailed to him in utter helplessness and pain. I knew he heard my cries, but Lord, *Why aren't you changing it?* During this time, his grace and mercy were abundant. Without him, I could not have survived the incredible pain."

She began to cling to God's promises, claiming those found in Joel 2:25 (NKJV), "I will restore to you the years the swarming locust has eaten," and Isaiah 49:25 (NKJV), "I will contend with him who contends with you, and I will save your children."

"I often went to these verses, and I would say them out loud and claim them because it gave me hope," she said. "Even though time had gone on and on, I would just return to these verses. *No, the Lord told me this, they are going to come back.*"

Feeling restless, Susan would walk outdoors to physically call out her pleas to the Lord aloud.

"Sometimes I would go out to the end of my driveway, and look for them, and just cry out for them and call them by name…I would just tell them, 'I'm waiting for you to come back!' I don't know what the neighbors thought," she said, chuckling a little. "But I didn't care. I wanted to do something physical to show that I was walking in faith and that I was waiting for them to come home."

Restoration

Twelve years after her divorce from Mark was finalized, Susan met Bill. His faith in her and in their love helped restore her sense of self, and things began to change.

"I think I changed when I met Bill too. He showed me he loved me for who I was, and he knew how sad I was for my boys, and he totally supported me and was compassionate. I think I was able to start letting those walls come down and start to trust again," she said.

Four years ago, Susan's prayers finally began to be answered. One day while at work, Susan received a text message from her youngest son, Jeremy.

"He just said, 'Mom, I want to meet you for supper, and I want to start over and put things behind us,'" she said. "We were both so scared, but we just talked. He said that he was sorry for all the things he'd said to me, and I told him I was sorry for my part in it, and from that day on we've just sort of slowly gotten closer together."

Not long afterward, Susan received a phone call from her daughter-in-law, Laurie, a Christian. She offered to bring Susan's two granddaughters over to spend some time with her. Slowly but surely, they began to build a relationship.

"I think she wanted to hear what my side of the story was," Susan said. "Not badmouthing anybody, but I think she needed to hear some truth about the situation."

At the time, Laurie and Tim were facing their own marital struggles, due in part to his unwillingness to deal with the pain of his parents' divorce.

"It came to a point where he went into a depression, and he couldn't get out of it," Susan recalled. It was at that point that

Laurie told him, "You need to get help, and you need to have a relationship with your mom."

After seeking out the advice of a pastor at their church, Tim agreed. In April 2011, he finally reunited with Susan.

"We just embraced each other," Susan said. They both cried and apologized for past actions and words.

It was a healing process for both of them: Susan had her son back, while Tim's marriage was revitalized.

"I think that was the beginning of Tim's marriage being restored—because he saw that by not having a relationship with me, and then listening to all that his dad had said, he found himself going down that same path and didn't want that," she said.

Help from Others

Looking back, Susan can see how the Lord brought people into her life—Bill, Laurie, a Christian counselor, her sister, even a Bible study with several parents estranged from their "prodigal" children—to come alongside her in her distress and provide perspective.

After years of feeling alone in her sorrow, Bill helped her regain her confidence.

"Bill gave me stability. And he gave me a guy's way of thinking. That's when my healing started," she said.

Laurie, too, was a direct link in Susan's restoration process.

"I just believe that Laurie is a godsend," Susan said. "Laurie is an answer to my prayers when I prayed for a wife for Tim. I prayed that God would give him a Christian wife, and he did. She just has a beautiful heart."

For Susan, relying on the promises of God and the comfort of others has been freeing.

"God can't work when we are trying to fix it ourselves," Susan said. "Freedom comes when we let go and allow him to change our circumstances. Letting go doesn't mean we love less, it means we are trusting him to do a better job."

Although Susan has yet to be reunited with her middle son, Andy, she continues to believe that he will find his way back to her, in time.

"I know he's already on his way back. I don't really know what's happening in his life. I hear a little bit about it. I just keep praying for him, and look for that day," Susan said.

She trusts God to take care of it, she said, because he's kept his promise to restore her relationships with her other sons.

"I have more trust now, because Tim's back and Jeremy's back—I have a trust in the Lord that I've never had before because they're back."

Over the years, that trust in the Lord has played a key role in her own healing process.

"I had to let go and just say, 'Lord, you do this.' Because in my power and my trying to fix it—it wasn't working," she said. "I couldn't have done it without him. I think I would have died— you know, that's how he carries you through. Many times you can't feel it, but he's there. And when I look back I can see that clearly. He heals you from the inside out."

Conclusion

Just as Bill, Laurie, and countless other people came alongside Susan, and just as the Christian chiropractor and a stranger came alongside Julie and Lisa, we as believers in Christ are called to step forward and help others even when they are someone outside our small circle of influence. If we strive to live our lives as Christ called us and as Paul encouraged us, at the end of our lives, we will remember times when we walked a mile in the shoes of Naomi and Ruth, having to rely upon and accept the assistance of fellow believers. And if we keep our eyes open and our hearts willing, we will remember times when we walked in the shoes of Boaz, wearing our Wonder Woman capes as we join with Jesus to swoop to the rescue of friends, strangers, and people we've never met in faraway lands.

Prayer

Lord, open our eyes, our ears, and our hearts to those around us. Remind us to respond when we see an unmet need and a hurting heart. Challenge us to use our time wisely and help us to order our priorities in our busy lives so that we are never too busy to say yes to your invitation. May we respond as the Samaritan instead of the passersby! And when it is our turn to accept assistance from a fellow Christian, help us to set aside pride and the deception of independence, and let us focus on you and what you are doing in our lives during that time. Remind each of us that we are loved by you—regardless of whether we are currently in the position of being rescued or are rescuing someone else. Amen.

Read Ruth 3:7–4:12.

1. Can you remember a time when God answered a prayer in an unexpected way? What were the results?

_____

_____

_____

2. The authors explained how sometimes we are the answer to someone else's prayers and sometimes we must rely on another's assistance for an answered prayer.

_____

_____

_____

a. Can you think of an example from your own life where you either assisted someone else or offered your assistance?

_____

_____

_____

b. What was it like to be on the giving or receiving side of helping?

_____

_____

_____

3. Psalm 27:14 [NLT] encourages us to "wait patiently for the Lord. Be brave and courageous. Yes, wait patiently for the Lord."

_____

_____

_____

a. Ruth, Naomi, and Susan had to wait on the Lord for their prayers to be answered. What prayers are you still waiting on answers to?

_____

_____

_____

b. *How can you continue to trust while you wait?*

_____

_____

_____

3. *Although at times we struggle as Susan did with questions regarding why things unfold the way they do, ultimately we can choose to stand on the promises of God while we wait. What promises can you cling to during your own waiting season?*

_____

_____

_____

7

Our Redemption

So Boaz took Ruth into his home, and she became his wife. When he slept with her, the Lord enabled her to become pregnant, and she gave birth to a son. Then the women of the town said to Naomi, "Praise the Lord, who has now provided a redeemer for your family! May this child be famous in Israel. May he restore your youth and care for you in your old age. For he is the son of your daughter-in-law who loves you and has been better to you than seven sons!"

—Ruth 4:13–15 (NLT)

My husband and I (Julie) recently purchased four plane tickets to fly our family to Idaho to visit my brother, his wife, and their new baby. I intended to redeem those credit card "reward points" I had been saving up for years. Of course, the red tape was so tangled, the process so complex, and the airline's rules so confusing that I eventually gave up. As I paid full price for the tickets, I grumpily thought to myself, *So much for redeeming reward points! All that work to save up points was worthless!*

In our American culture, the concept of redemption has been hijacked by commercialism. Credit card companies, retail businesses, and everyone with something to sell offers reward points, loyalty cards, and a variety of other gimmicks so consumers who "buy now" can "redeem a reward" later. Of course, the rules and strings attached to the reward are often so burdensome or restrictive that many people simply give up without ever gaining the reward.

Our culture has so intertwined the idea of redemption with red tape, extra work, and strings attached that our understanding of redemption has become synonymous with hidden rules and traps. We often then transfer our understanding and secular experiences with redemption to God's concept of redemption. God doesn't play the strings-attached game with redemption. When a business offers reward points, it is because it benefits the business. Businesses reap a benefit by dangling the carrot of a future redemption and benefit further when people cannot satisfy the requirements to actually receive the promised redemption. As Christians, it's important to set aside our secular ideas of redemption as we explore God's view of the concept.

God Restores Our Futures

When God used Boaz to redeem and restore Ruth and Naomi, he did not simply return them to approximately the same position of wealth and security they enjoyed in Moab. Instead, God went above and beyond their wildest dreams!

God returned Naomi to her homeland after she had to flee to the country of Moab years earlier to escape a famine. He restored Naomi's legacy and lineage through the birth of a new grandson, Obed. In fact, Naomi's redemption was so great that the townswomen exclaimed:

"Blessed be God! He didn't leave you without family to carry on your life. May this baby grow up to be famous in Israel! He'll make you young again! He'll take care of you in old age. And this daughter-in-law who has brought him into the world and loves you so much, why, she's worth more to you than seven sons!" Naomi took the baby and held him in her arms, cuddling him, cooing over him, waiting on him hand and foot. The neighborhood women started calling him "Naomi's baby boy!" (Ruth 4:14–17 [MSG])

Yet while the redemption of Naomi is both beautiful and complete, it is Ruth's redemption that is overwhelming in its scope.

God Redeems Our Past

I (Julie) have an acquaintance who married an Englishman and moved to his home country. About a year after she moved, I asked her mother how she was adjusting. She told me that her daughter loved England, but would often find herself suddenly becoming homesick over a million tiny cultural differences. Although the United States and England share a similar language and interwoven histories, differences in slang, food, and perspective caught this woman off guard in unexpected moments. As I pondered Ruth's experience in following Naomi to Judah, I was reminded of the stories this mother told of her daughter's adjustment. For Ruth, the adjustment must have been even more difficult as she followed Naomi into a land, culture, and people who had been bitter enemies of her own people for generations. Despite this hurdle, Ruth declared her intention to leave the gods of Moab and follow the one true God of Israel.

As chapter six discussed, someone becomes Jewish only through birth or conversion. But God did much more than simply accept Ruth as an Israelite through conversion; instead, he went further and inserted Ruth into the direct lineage of Jesus Christ through her marriage to Boaz. Think of that: *Ruth became an ancestor of Christ.* The final verses of Ruth detail how Ruth and Boaz's son, Obed, became the father of Jesse, who was the father of King David (Ruth 4:18–22 [NLT]). The lineage of Christ is recounted both in the Old and New Testaments in several locations to varying degrees of completeness, yet even in the most complete accountings of Christ's lineage, only five women are identified by name. Amazingly, Ruth is one of them (Matthew 1:2–6).

If a hated Moabite was redeemed and incorporated into the direct lineage of Christ, what does that tell us about God's ability to redeem us from our pasts? As incredible as it is to see a Moabitess listed in the lineage of Christ, God does one better: Ruth is one of only two women with a book in the Bible bearing her name. God's overwhelming redemption of Ruth reveals the same tender mercy and love he has for you and I.

I (Kendra) grew up in a loving Christian home but, like many girls and young women in our culture, mistook sexual intimacy for love. I gave my heart and body to a young man who did not return my affections, thinking that if I did, it would draw him to me, and that through that sexual action, he would love me.

Nothing could have been further from the truth, but as a young woman, I was easily deceived, believing that such close physical intimacy could only mean that he returned the love I felt for him. I remember when I finally started to realize that I was simply being used, that the love I felt would not be returned. I was devastated; it was the worst emotional pain I've ever experienced and one that I was ashamed to share with anyone else. I was embarrassed for anyone to know what I'd done and how naïve I'd been, so I kept it to myself.

As the years went on, I engaged in more ungodly relationships, but no longer suffered a broken heart when they ended. I was hardened to the realities of what a sexual relationship outside of what God designed could cost me. It wasn't until I was in my early twenties and returned to the Lord that I realized how hard my heart had become.

Over the course of a few years, God began to reveal to me the unhealthy patterns that I started as a teenager, attracting men physically, thinking that was the way to get them to fall in love with me. God took back my heart from that first young man who had broken it so many years before and healed it. He then held it, and as I learned to trust Jesus, he became the love of my life. He also broke the ties that had been created with each of those men through sex. As my heart began to soften again, I began to see myself the way God did, as a young woman who deserved the love, admiration, and respect of a young man apart from a physical relationship. God showed me that I had value and so much more to bring to a relationship than just sex. During this time I didn't date, choosing instead to spend time with my friends and family, growing in the Lord.

When I was twenty-four, God brought a young man into my life who became a dear friend to me, who valued my walk with the Lord, and who wanted to know me as a person. When we began dating and I told him about my past, he couldn't believe that I had been that person. He didn't care what I had done, and when he said he loved me, I believed him. There's nothing else that could have changed my heart the way that Jesus did to prepare me for this man who soon after became my husband. It was only through God's redemptive grace that my heart was healed and made whole again.

There is nothing in our past that God cannot redeem. A good example to consider is Saul, who was a Pharisee and did not believe that Jesus Christ was the Messiah. In fact, Saul was one of the most vocal, dangerous persecutors of early Christians. The portrayal of Saul witnessing the death of Stephen, a man who knew and followed Christ, is chilling:

> *As the rocks rained down, Stephen prayed, "Master Jesus, take my life." Then he knelt down, praying loud enough for everyone to hear, "Master, don't blame them for this sin"—his last words. Then he died. Saul was right there, congratulating the killers. (Acts 7:59–8:1 [MSG])*

We learn that Saul didn't stop with the murder of Stephen, as Acts 8:3 (MSG) continues, "And Saul just went wild, devastating the church, entering house after house after house, dragging men and women off to jail."

Yet in the midst of Saul's rampage against Christians, God stepped into Saul's life on the road to Damascus.

All this time Saul was breathing down the necks of the Master's disciples, out for the kill. He went to the Chief Priest and got arrest warrants to take to the meeting places in Damascus so that if he found anyone there belonging to the Way, whether men or women, he could arrest them and bring them to Jerusalem.

He set off. When he got to the outskirts of Damascus, he was suddenly dazed by a blinding flash of light. As he fell to the ground, he heard a voice: "Saul, Saul, why are you out to get me?"

He said, "Who are you, Master?"

"I am Jesus, the One you're hunting down. I want you to get up and enter the city. In the city you'll be told what to do next."

> *His companions stood there dumbstruck—they could hear the sound, but couldn't see anyone—while Saul,*

picking himself up off the ground, found himself stone-blind. They had to take him by the hand and lead him into Damascus. He continued blind for three days. He ate nothing, drank nothing. (Acts 9:1–9 [MSG])

Once in Damascus, Saul's sight was restored and he became a follower of Christ. In fact, Saul created a lot of confusion in the Jewish community because he *immediately* began to preach that Jesus was the Messiah. Saul's former allies, after their initial confusion, try to kill Saul for his changed heart and vocal preaching.

What does God do with this former murderous, scheming man, a man who celebrated the killing of Stephen, a personal friend of Jesus Christ? Most of us are more familiar with Saul under his Roman name of Paul—the same Paul who, most biblical scholars agree, wrote at least thirteen and maybe fourteen books contained in the New Testament! God took a man on a murderous rampage, struck him blind, changed his heart, and then used him to write a significant portion of the New Testament. If God can use such a man to spread the message of Jesus Christ to millions of people over two thousand years, imagine what he can do with you and me.

Sarah's Story

When Sarah* became a teen mom at seventeen, she was following in the footsteps of her mother and grandmother. When she divorced her first husband, she followed in their footsteps, as well.

By the time she was twenty-three, Sarah was a single mom with three children under the age of six to raise. And although it was hard, it was a role she felt comfortable with—after all, it's what she was used to.

Having grown up mostly fatherless, Sarah wasn't used to seeing good marriages modeled in real life. Her biological father was never around, and although she was adopted by her mother's second husband, he also had little involvement in her life after the death of Sarah's baby sister when Sarah was eight. Since her grandparents were also divorced, Sarah grew up in the midst of a grandmother, aunt, mom, and mom's best friend who were all single mothers.

"It was just all these single mothers around," she said. "I lived with my mom, and boyfriends were just that—they were boyfriends, they didn't have any power in the family. My mom said, specifically, 'You don't trust a man.'"

When Sarah became pregnant at age seventeen, she and her son's father decided to get married. Although she wanted it to work out, his inability to handle adult responsibilities and increasingly volatile temper led to the marriage's ending.

"He just couldn't stop seeing other women. He couldn't stop drinking and using drugs. He was just very young and not ready to be an adult and take care of kids," she said. "He just didn't have the skills. There were a lot of verbal tantrums and yelling at me, and by the time we split up, I was very afraid of him. One time he was screaming at me and I could feel his teeth on my hand. It just got scary."

They split up when the kids were six, three and one years old, and it was easier in some ways—she had more money, and she no longer had anything to fear—but it was harder too.

"It was difficult," she said. "I remember being on my face and crying out to God. I didn't know Jesus. I didn't know God, but I just prayed to him to send me angels. It was just too hard. And he did, he sent people into my life."

When Sarah heard that a friend of hers wanted to go to church, she asked if she could go along. Her friend agreed, and Sarah began to cautiously explore faith in God.

"I went to church with her and just started learning. People were nice and there were classes for my kids, and people wanting to teach them and love them. I remember thinking, *Wow, this is great stuff*," she said.

By this time, Sarah had met someone new. But although she and her then-boyfriend Ben were in a serious relationship, he didn't show any interest in church.

"We were living together, and we had a child together, but we had no example of marriage in our family to follow. We had no blueprint, no map, and so we were struggling. And then God told me in church one day, 'You aren't married to him, so you shouldn't act like you are,'" Sarah recalled. "I was so convicted. I left crying. I didn't want to stay there because I was bawling my eyes out."

When she went home, she told Ben, "I think God sent you to me and that we're meant to be together, but I think we got off on the wrong path. I don't think we're doing it right, so either we're getting married or we're breaking up."

A month later, they decided to get married. After meeting with the pastor for premarital counseling, Ben agreed to go to church. One day, while attending a guest speaker, Ben ended up going to the front for prayer.

"I could feel the power of God, heavy, almost like a breath," Sarah said. "I told the Lord, 'I knew you were real, God, I knew it.' That encounter with the Lord was life-changing for him. "

As Christians, Sarah and Ben were determined to set a new example for their children. Having experienced redemption, they wanted to continue that heritage for their family.

For Sarah, it was a struggle. Having grown up in a female-dominated house where her mom's word was unquestioned, compromise was difficult.

"My mom taught me based on what she had learned and what she felt was safe and right," Sarah said. "She didn't teach me not to depend on a man to be mean, she wanted me to be safe. Her father had left her mother alone and my father had left her alone."

When she felt the Lord leading her to quit her job for a season in life, she struggled. In her mind, she could hear her mom's voice, telling her that it was her house, her kids, and that she shouldn't count on a man.

But her willingness to be obedient to the Lord has made a huge difference in her marriage, she said.

"That has saved us—seriously, that has saved our marriage. Because if I were working, I would think I could do it myself. I would think, 'I'm getting my own apartment, I don't need to compromise with you,'" she said.

Although Sarah didn't grow up seeing healthy relationships, she's worked hard to compromise with her husband, even though it sometimes goes against how she was raised.

"To learn to depend on him actually felt like I was betraying my family," she said. "And I thought, if this doesn't work out, I'm in big trouble because I depended on a man and let a man parent my children. You know, I did all the wrong things according to what my family would say is the right thing to do."

In the midst of her battles, when the ghosts of old habits or feelings arise, Sarah holds tight to Isaiah 54:17 (NKJV):

"No weapon formed against you shall prosper, And every tongue which rises against you in judgment You shall condemn. This is the heritage of the servants of the Lord, And their righteousness is from Me," says the Lord.

"When you're constantly breaking through old junk and that old junk comes up again and you think, 'Why are we still doing this? Why is this still happening? Why does this still knock me out?' It doesn't matter, this is old stuff, and no weapon formed against you shall prosper. And that has been helpful because these weapons *will* be formed against us. The attacks *will* come. Those old attacks, 'You are a failure. You are not smart. You are not a good parent. You will never be a good parent. You did not do the right thing.' They are old lies. But I can use those as opportunities to grow in my faith," she said.

Not only has Sarah's redemption and restoration paid off in her own life, but in her children's lives as well.

"Of the men in our family, my oldest son is the first boy to graduate from high school, he's the first to go to college, he's the first to be drug- and alcohol-free and never have gone to jail," she said. "I can see it even more in my children, as they grow—I know that I'm going to see God through them and that they're going to overcome these things. They won't have some of the battles that I had or their dad had because God delivered them."

Conclusion

God is the redeemer of our pasts and the restorer of our futures. Romans 8:28 states it beautifully: "And we know that in all things God works for the good of those who love him, who have been called according to his purpose." If God could redeem a hated Moabitess and place her within the lineage of Christ, if he could alter the life of a murderer bent on single-handedly destroying the early church and invite him to write a large portion of the New Testament, is there anything you or I can do that is beyond redemption? No. Nothing is beyond redemption. Nothing is beyond restoration. Nothing is impossible for God.

What troubles from your past is God waiting to redeem? What hurts is he asking you to turn over to him so that he might restore your future? Kendra and Sarah were able to turn to God and hand him their pain. In return, they found God waiting for them as they endeavored to set the past aside and start living according to God's Word. Did you know that God is waiting for you, too? He desires to redeem and restore those things you believe to be lost so that you can fulfill your true potential as a child of God. When we are willing to share our personal stories of how God met us in the hardest, most difficult places in our lives, we give hope and courage to those around us. There is power in our stories of redemption, restoration, and God's provision in our times of need—regardless of how small, dull, embarrassing, or shameful we label our lives. Never underestimate the power of God to use your life story to encourage and transform those around you.

Prayer

Lord, thank you for redeemed pasts and restored futures. Thank you that there is nothing you cannot forgive and that not one of us has a past so shameful that you cannot reclaim our future. Thank you for the hope we have as we look at the biblical examples of murderers, prostitutes, and despised foreigners you chose to use, despite their pasts, in mighty ways to change thousands of lives. Reveal to each of us what areas in our pasts we need to bring to you for healing and for redemption. As we bring you our past, restore our future. Give us new hope as we move forward into a deepening relationship with you and as we break the chains of the past. Amen.

Your Turn

Read Ruth 4:13–22.

1. *What areas of your life has God redeemed? What, if anything, may God still need to redeem from your past?*

_____

_____

_____

2. *Like Sarah, are there struggles you have faced and overcome from your past after starting a relationship with Jesus?*

_____

_____

_____

3. First Peter 5:10 [NLT] states, "In his kindness God called you to share in his eternal glory by means of Christ Jesus. So after you have suffered a little while, he will restore, support, and strengthen you, and he will place you on a firm foundation." This passage promises us that after we've suffered a little while, God will restore, support, and strengthen us. What encouragement can you take away today from this scripture regarding a difficult or challenging situation you may currently be facing?

_____

_____

_____

4. As you look to the future, what are some areas of your life you believe God can and will restore?

_____

_____

_____

8

Your Action Steps

I (Kendra) have been part of church since I was a baby. In fact, my parents like to tell me that the first time they ever took me out of the house as a three-week-old newborn was to attend a tent revival meeting, so I feel like being in a group of believers is in my blood. I have heard countless messages and wonderful sermons throughout the years, but I think some of the most impactful church gatherings I have attended involved people sharing their story. Often the stories revolved around how God showed up in the midst of something difficult or challenging in their lives, or how God moved in a miraculous way. Woven into each story—no matter how different the extenuating circumstances—God was characterized as faithful and true. And despite the unique circumstances of each person's tale, each story gave glory to God, encouraging and building the faith of those listening. There is nothing as powerful as hearing what God has done in another person's life.

Throughout the Bible, God used people's stories as a way to instruct us, explain things to us, and show us more of his character. In fact, rather than focusing on impersonal rules and regulations to explain his message, Jesus used parables and stories to explain doctrine, teach, and encourage people throughout the New Testament. It is no different for us today. God is still using the testimonies of his people to share his love and redemption with those who are willing to listen. Our stories build up not only our own faith, but the faith of others, as well.

By now, you've followed the stories of Ruth and Naomi, read other women's testimonies and answered questioned about your own life. What's the next step? It's our firm belief that your willingness to tell your own story to others is one of the most important action steps you can take. The apostle John wrote to the early churches, foretelling what would happen in the future through a vision he was given:

> *Then I heard a loud voice shouting across the heavens, "It has come at last—salvation and power and the Kingdom of our God, and the authority of his Christ." (Rev. 12:10 [NLT])*

Let's consider this for a moment: Our authority over situations, feelings, and actions all comes through Christ. In him, we are able to take captive everything that does not line up with the Word of God. We can have victory in our lives because of his salvation and the power that we have received. The passage continues,

> *For the accuser of our brothers and sisters has been thrown down to earth—the one who accuses them before our God day and night." [Rev. 12:10 [NLT])*

We have an enemy of our souls who loves to accuse us before God the Father. He doesn't just like to remind us why we're incapable, unworthy, and unlovable, he likes to tell God about it too. Day and night, he lays out all of our shortcomings before God. Sounds pretty impossible to overcome, right? It might be, except that we are the given the key to our victory:

*And they have defeated him by the blood of the Lamb
and by their testimony. (Revelations 12:11[NLT])*

Did you catch that? We have the ability to overcome Satan. We have the ability to overcome what he tries to tell God about us and what he tries to whisper or sometimes shout into our own lives. We have a way to silence his lies. He is defeated first by the blood of the Lamb, Jesus, whose death and resurrection has washed away our sins, making us right with God the Father. This sacrifice was God's action step toward us; all we do is accept it. But the second part of this verse speaks to the action step that we must take in return: sharing our testimony. Our testimony is powerful because it speaks of God's redeeming grace in our lives, reminds us of who we are in Christ, and is a witness to those around us. It speaks to others in the midst of whatever they are facing, reminding them that there is a God who loves them, who will see them through their difficulty, and who wants to redeem the most damning of stories. There is power in our testimony and that is our action step in defeating the enemy, because the exact thing that Satan accuses us of—past sins, mistakes we've made, or ways we don't measure up—Jesus has redeemed. Our story in Christ will always trump anything the enemy could bring against us. Romans 8:28 (NLT) says, "And we know that God causes everything to work together for the good of those who love God and are called according to His purpose for them." Everything that has ever happened in our lives, God can turn to good and transform into a testimony that will bring him glory.

Your Story

In this chapter, instead of offering another woman's testimony, we are asking you to share yours. We believe everyone has a story, but if you need help refining yours or getting ideas, look back at some of the questions you answered throughout this book. It may give you insight into pieces of your testimony that are valuable to share. There is no right or wrong way to tell your story. Whatever it is, it has value to God and it is worth repeating.

Here are a few questions to get you started:

- Are there any specific stories or events from your life that speak to some of the major themes we've discussed (honesty with God, trusting God, faith in action, redemption)? Which one(s) stand out to you the most?

_____

_____

_____

- How did that circumstance or event affect your relationship with others? With God?

_____

_____

_____

- How much did you have to rely on God during that time? Did you feel like you could trust him to take care of you, or was it a struggle?

_____

_____

_____

- Were there any particular verse(s) from the Bible that you held on to during this time in your life?

_____

_____

_____

- Looking back, what about that time in your life stands out to you the most?

_____

_____

_____

- What was the outcome of this experience? What did it teach you?

_____

_____

_____

- Do you feel like God has redeemed you through this experience?

_____

_____

_____

As we were writing this book, we had many discussions about the personal stories and examples we shared within each chapter, and how vulnerable our honesty made us feel. We struggled at times with the idea of sharing so much of ourselves with other people, even those who wouldn't know us personally, and what they would think or say about us. We finally came to two conclusions to combat the hesitancy we felt, and they might help you as well. The first is that writing out your testimony—at least initially—is simply an exercise between you and God. It's a chance to be honest and real with the only person who will never hurt you and is completely safe—Jesus. Once we have allowed him access to every area of our lives, we can find his healing, grace, and mercy available to us, no matter our story. The second conclusion is something we mentioned earlier but bears repeating: There is power to defeat the enemy by speaking or writing our story and retelling what God has done. It not only edifies us, but builds others' faith as well.

With that being said, we also believe that discernment is needed when sharing your story. You may want to start with just a good friend or spouse. If you are willing to go further, begin by sharing in a small group or wherever you are most comfortable. We also understand and want to encourage you to realize that there may be times God asks you to step out in sharing your story, perhaps with a stranger or a group of people, and our goal in this book is to help inspire you to be obedient to God. We don't deny that you may feel vulnerable at times—we certainly have—or that people will not hurt you in the process, because they may. But we hold fast to the belief that God is big enough to handle every situation, loves us beyond comprehension, and is pleased with us when we obey him.

Sharing Your Story

Small-Group Setting

One effective way to start your own "Ruth Experience" is by gathering a group of women and meeting on a regular basis. This could include (but is certainly not limited to) women from your church, neighborhood, or workplace.

General Suggestions

- Meetings can happen in the home, local coffee shop or any-where else a small group would feel comfortable meeting.

- Groups can meet on a weekly or biweekly basis, however often you would like and any day of the week, just plan on being consistent.

Preparation: Before the Group Starts

- Decide how long your group will last. Will you meet for six weeks or eight?
- Start by choosing a book that can be read at home and discussed together when you meet.
- Lay out a schedule of chapters to be read and the dates for each meeting so women know what kind of time they are committing to investing. How many chapters will you read and discuss each time?
- Please note: It's helpful to give as much information up front to the women you would like to invite so they can make the best decision if it will work for their schedules or not.

Action: A Sample Meeting

Here's an example structure of the time element. You've planned to meet on Saturday mornings from 8:00 a.m.–9:30 a.m.

- 8:00–8:15—Women arrive
- 8:15–9:00—Book discussion
- 9:00–9:30—Prayer requests, time for prayer, and closing

Good to Know

We have found that although you do not need to be rigid about the time, it is good to have a general schedule to follow, as it gives women some idea about how the group will function each week. As you know, women are busy, so it's important to be respectful of others' time by beginning and ending on time. We all appreciate knowing what we are agreeing to do before saying yes to something. We believe that if you start meeting regularly, you will have ample opportunity to share your story and be encouraged when others share theirs as well.

I (Julie) still remember vividly the Sunday morning when a woman named Kate walked across the church sanctuary to invite me, a new attendee sitting by myself, to sit by her during the service. My husband and I had been attending for several months and were in that awkward stage of belonging but not really having friends. My husband was on the worship team with Kate's husband, so I often sat by myself during a good portion of the service. As I sat by Kate, she told me that she had recently formed a small Bible study and invited me to join. I barely knew Kate, and although the other women in the study were from the same church, they were also strangers. I joined that small study of six, expecting to meet in Kate's kitchen, read books, and share prayer requests. What I could not have expected were the ways in which I would be allowed an intimate glimpse into these other women's lives as they poured out joy, sorrow, anger, and hope during prayer time. As we grew in our relationships with God, we also grew in our relationships with one another. We became spiritual litmus tests for one another—encouraging during hard times, gently holding one another accountable, crying, laughing, and sharing our lives together through prayer. After Kate died, we continued to meet weekly.

After approximately five years of meeting together, we each began to feel a restlessness. Although we remained close friends, our Bible study did not have the vibrancy it once had, and we each privately considered disbanding the study. We met to discuss what we were going to do, and it was at that meeting that we realized we had reached a point in our individual Christian walks where we needed to start pouring out into the lives of other women. Instead of disbanding, we decided to make our Bible study into our ministry. We choose a funny, inviting book. We each made lists of women from our neighborhoods, workplaces, schools, and church. We put together our calendar of meeting dates, then started inviting women. As soon as we shifted the focus of our study into a ministry to other women, the restlessness left. We've now been ministering to other women through our Bible study for an additional four years, and I've been sharing in the lives of countless other women through weekly prayer requests for almost ten years. When I accepted that invitation to join Kate's study, I had no idea how my walk with God would mature and strengthen as I walked through life with my sisters in Christ. It is in the sharing of our lives and our testimonies with fellow Christian women that we grow in faith and our relationship with Christ.

Large-Group Setting

Another way to create a "Ruth Experience" on a larger scale is to host a one-time women's event at your church or home.

Preparation: Before the Event

- Start by gathering a few women who could help you plan the evening.
- Ask two to three women to share a part of their testimony about how God has made a difference in their lives. Each woman is given a certain amount of time to share.

- It is good to have an emcee or two to host the event, even possibly giving a brief explanation as to why it is important to share testimonies with others.

- You may want to have refreshments available.

Action: A Sample Event

A possible schedule for the evening could be as follows:
- 6:30 p.m.–7:00 p.m.—Refreshments and fellowship.

- 7:00 p.m.–8:10 p.m.—Welcome the women to the evening, briefly explaining about the importance of sharing testimonies with others. Have three women on a panel share their testimonies, with each woman taking twenty minutes to share.

- 8:10 p.m.–8:30 p.m.—Offer prayer for the women who are in the audience. Have a few women available to pray with and for them.

- 8:30 p.m.—Finish by closing in prayer.

Of course, this is just one example. Feel free to get creative and utilize the talents of others in planning an exciting event.

Conclusion

We are so thankful that you have joined us on this journey. We pray that through these chapters you have been able to see God's redemptive story come alive in your own life and story. We hope that you realize the importance of your own story and understand just how unique and special God has made you. May you now feel empowered to share what God has done with those around you. May your story be used to encourage and equip other women as you intentionally seek out opportunities to share with others. May you realize that your story is really not about you, but about the God of the universe, reaching down to offer each one of us the love and redemption we need in this life. And finally, may it give you renewed hope as you continue your own journey with God, the courage to continue to share it with others, and the faith to believe that he who began a good work in you will see it through to completion.

Prayer

Lord, thank you that you have individually sought each one of us out and invited us into a personal relationship with you. Thank you that you take us beyond friendship and into a sisterhood with fellow Christian women as we share our testimonies and our lives. Bring at least one "sister" into the life of each woman reading this book. Bring to mind, even now, the face of a woman who might be struggling, hurting, or new to Christianity, that we might be the one to reach out a hand of sisterhood. Give wisdom and discernment to each of us as we consider sharing testimonies that involve difficult past experiences; we acknowledge that with powerful stories comes vulnerability. Protect our vulnerabilities and shine light into the dark places of our lives so that the devil forever loses his ability to beat us up over that experience. Take each and every experience from our past that are meant for our personal destruction and use it to show others your redeeming love and power in and over our lives. Thank you, Lord, that you are raising up a sisterhood of women who support, lovingly correct, and laugh, cry, and cheer one another on as we walk through this life together. Amen!

Your Turn

1. *What is the next step God is asking you to take now that you have completed this book?*

_____

_____

_____

2. *Who is a trusted person that you can share your testimony, or even just a portion of it, within a safe environment?*

_____

_____

_____

3. *Mark 16:15 [NLT] says, "And then he [Jesus] told them, 'Go into all the world and preach the Good News to everyone.'" How does sharing what God has done in our lives accomplish Jesus's great commission to preach the good news to everyone?*

_____

_____

_____

4. What are some final thoughts or lessons that God has taught you through this process that you want to remember?

_____

_____

_____

Now all glory to God, who is able, through his mighty power at work within us, to accomplish infinitely more than we might ask or think. Glory to him in the church and in Christ Jesus through all generations forever and ever! Amen. —Ephesians 3:20–21 (NLT)

End Notes

- Dictionary.com Unabridged, s.v. "pride" accessed July 13, 2012, http://dictionary.reference.com/browse/pride.

- 1 Samuel 1; Exodus 2:23; Genesis 16:7

- Dictionary.com Unabridged, s.v. "degenerate," accessed July 13, 2012, http://dictionary.reference.com/browse/degenerate

- *Connotates that some names have been changed.

Made in the USA
Middletown, DE
16 November 2016